Problems of Knowledge and Freedom

Problems of Knowledge and Freedom

THE RUSSELL LECTURES

— BY —

NOAM CHOMSKY

33484

PANTHEON BOOKS

A DIVISION OF RANDOM HOUSE, NEW YORK

ISBN: 0-394- 47260-8

Library of Congress Catalog Card Number: 76-162557

The two lectures included in this book were originally published, in slightly different form, in the *Cambridge Review,* Cambridge, England, in 1971.

Manufactured in the United States of America

3 5 7 9 8 6 4 2

FIRST EDITION

Contents

— *Introduction* —

THE TASK OF a liberal education, Bertrand Russell once wrote, is "to give a sense of the value of things other than domination, to help to create wise citizens of a free community, and through the combination of citizenship with liberty in individual creativeness to enable men to give to human life that splendor which some few have shown that it can achieve."[1] Among those few who have shown, in this century, the splendor that human life can achieve in individual creativeness and the struggle for liberty, Bertrand Russell holds a place of honor. In reflecting on his life and achievement, the temptation to quote Russell's own words is quite irresistible.

> Those whose lives are fruitful to themselves, to their friends, or to the world are inspired by hope and sustained by joy: they see in imagination the things that might be and the way in which they are to be brought into existence. In their private rela-

[1] *Power: A New Social Analysis* (New York: W. W. Norton & Company, 1938), p. 305.

tions they are not pre-occupied with anxiety lest they should lose such affection and respect as they receive: they are engaged in giving affection and respect freely, and the reward comes of itself without their seeking. In their work they are not haunted by jealousy of competitors, but are concerned with the actual matter that has to be done. In politics, they do not spend time and passion defending unjust privileges of their class or nation, but they aim at making the world as a whole happier, less cruel, less full of conflict between rival greeds, and more full of human beings whose growth has not been dwarfed and stunted by oppression.[2]

When this description of how life should be lived was written, Russell had already changed the course of modern thought with his monumental contributions to philosophy and logic, and was facing obloquy and imprisonment for his determined opposition to a war that he could not accept as just or necessary. Still to come was half a century of creative achievement, not only in thought and inquiry but in an unending, unyielding effort to make the world happier and less cruel. While Russell's intellectual achievements remain a delight to the inquiring mind, it is what Erich Fromm perceptively calls his renewal of the "Promethean function in his own life"[3] that will continue to inspire those who hope to be citizens of a free community.

[2] Bertrand Russell, *Proposed Roads to Freedom—Anarchy, Socialism and Syndicalism* (New York: Henry Holt & Co., 1919), pp. 186–87.
[3] "Prophets and Priests," in A. J. Ayer et al., *Bertrand Russell: Philosopher of the Century,* ed. Ralph Schoenman (Boston: Little Brown and Company, 1968), p. 72.

I need not review here the harassment, the ridicule and abuse that Russell endured in the course of these efforts, the shameful suppression and distortion, the revilement by apologists for the criminal violence of the state. One can only hope that this was more than compensated by the deep respect of decent people throughout the world. I will mention only two small examples. A friend, a young Asian scholar, visiting a tiny island near Okinawa a few months ago, stopped at the home of a farmer who has become the leader of a struggle to free their land from military domination—the movement a curious blend of Christianity and traditional beliefs with a strong populist strain. On a wall, he noticed a poster in Japanese which read: "Which road is the correct one, which is just? Is it the way of Confucius, of the Buddha, of Jesus Christ, Gandhi, Bertrand Russell? Or is it the way of Alexander the Great, Genghis Khan, Hitler, Mussolini, Napoleon, Tojo, President Johnson?"

A second case: Heinz Brandt, on his release from an East German prison, went to visit Russell, whose protest, including the return of a peace medal awarded by the German Democratic Republic, led to his release. As he left, Brandt writes, Russell stood at the door "looking very lonely, very old, [waving] to us with a moving, infinitely human gesture."[4] While Brandt has a more personal reason than most to be thankful for Russell's humanity, his gratitude can be shared by all of those who value reason, liberty, and justice, who are captivated by Russell's vision of "the world that we must seek,"

[4] Heinz Brandt, *The Search for a Third Way* (Garden City, N.Y.: Doubleday & Company, 1970), p. 305.

a world in which the creative spirit is alive, in which life is an adventure full of joy and hope, based rather upon the impulse to construct than upon the desire to retain what we possess or to seize what is possessed by others. It must be a world in which affection has free play, in which love is purged of the instinct for domination, in which cruelty and envy have been dispelled by happiness and the unfettered development of all the instincts that build up life and fill it with mental delights.[5]

Russell sought not only to interpret the world but also to change it. I imagine that he would have agreed with Marx's admonition that to change the world is "the real task." I would not presume to assess or even to try to record his achievement in interpreting or changing the world. To several generations, mine among them, Russell has been an inspiring figure, in the problems he posed and the causes he championed, in his insights as well as what is left unfinished. In these lectures, I will consider a few of the problems to which Russell addressed himself in his efforts to interpret and change the world. The selection of topics reflects my personal interests; others might choose, with equal justice, to emphasize different aspects of his work. I will consider primarily Russell's final summation, in his work of the 1940s, of his many years of inquiry into problems of knowledge, and his social and political thought—expressed in action as well —at about the time of World War I and in the last years of his life.

Is there a common thread running through Russell's enormously varied studies, which, taken as a whole,

[5] *Proposed Roads to Freedom,* p. 212.

touch on virtually every question of vital human concern? Is there, in particular, a link between his philosophical and political convictions? It is by no means obvious that a given person's efforts, in such separate domains, must derive from a common source or be at all tightly linked. Perhaps, nevertheless, one can discern some common elements in Russell's endeavor to discover the conditions of human knowledge and the conditions of human freedom. One point of contact I will discuss briefly in the final paragraphs of the first lecture and the beginning section of the second: the "humanistic conception" of man's intrinsic nature and creative potential that Russell formulates, as he places himself in a tradition of great richness and undiminished promise.

Publisher's Note

The following are the first Russell Lectures, originally presented by Noam Chomsky at Trinity College, Cambridge, in early 1971. The lectures have been slightly revised for presentation in this book.

Problems of Knowledge and Freedom

— 1 —

On Interpreting the World

A CENTRAL PROBLEM of interpreting the world is determining how, in fact, human beings proceed to do so. It is the study of the interaction between a particular, biologically given, complex system—the human mind—and the physical and social world. In the work in which he summarizes a lifetime of concern with this problem, Bertrand Russell asks "how comes it that human beings, whose contacts with the world are brief and personal and limited, are nevertheless able to know as much as they do know?"[1] Studying the relation between individual experience and the general body of knowledge, commonsense and scientific, Russell explores the limits of empiricism and tries to determine how it is possible to attain human knowledge; in particular, he attempts to discover the principles of nondemonstrative inference that justify scientific inference, "in addition to induction if not in place of it." He concludes that "part of empiricist theory

[1] *Human Knowledge: Its Scope and Limits* (New York: Simon & Schuster, 1948), p. v.

appears to be true without any qualification," namely, that "words which I can understand derive their meaning from my experience . . . [with] . . . no need to admit any exceptions whatever." Another part, he concludes, is untenable. We need certain principles of inference that "cannot be logically deduced from facts of experience. Either, therefore, we know something independently of experience, or science is moonshine." His investigation of prescientific knowledge, the knowledge that precedes systematic reflection on the principles of inference, leads to a similar result. His conclusions nevertheless retain "what we may call an empiricist 'flavour' ": though our knowledge of the underlying principles, "in so far as we do know them, cannot be based upon experience," nevertheless "all their verifiable consequences are such as experience will confirm."[2]

We might add that careful efforts to develop an empiricist theory of common-sense or scientific knowledge have generally led to somewhat similar conclusions. For example, David Hume concludes:

> But though animals learn many parts of their knowledge from observation, there are also many parts of it, which they derive from the original hand of nature; which much exceed the share of capacity they possess on ordinary occasions; and in which they improve, little or nothing, by the longest practice and experience. These we denominate Instincts, and are so apt to admire as something very extraordinary, and inexplicable by all the disquisitions of human understanding. But our wonder will, perhaps, cease or diminish, when we consider, that the experimental reasoning itself, which we

[2] *Ibid.,* pp. 522, 524, 526–27.

possess in common with beasts, and on which the whole conduct of life depends, is nothing but a species of instinct or mechanical power, that acts in us unknown to ourselves; and in its chief operations, is not directed by any such relations or comparisons of ideas, as are the proper objects of our intellectual faculties. Though the instinct be different, yet still it is an instinct, which teaches a man to avoid the fire; as much as that, which teaches a bird, with such exactness, the art of incubation, and the whole economy and order of its nursery.[3]

More recent efforts to develop an empiricist theory of acquisition of knowledge also reach conclusions not unlike Russell's. Thus Willard V. O. Quine, though he begins with concepts that seem very narrow and restricted, concludes finally that the innate system of properties (the "quality space") that underlies induction may have an abstract character, and that there are, furthermore, "as yet unknown innate structures, additional to mere quality space, that are needed in language-learning [and, presumably, other forms of learning as well] ... to get the child over this great hump that lies beyond ostension, or induction."[4] When Quine adds further that by "behaviorism" he refers only to "the insistence upon couching all criteria in observation terms" and eventually making sense of all conjectures

[3] *An Enquiry Concerning Human Understanding,* in David Hume, *Enquiries Concerning the Human Understanding and Concerning the Principles of Morals,* ed. L. A. Selby-Bigge, 2nd ed. (Oxford: Clarendon Press, 1902), p. 108.
[4] "Linguistics and Philosophy," in Sidney Hook, ed., *Language and Philosophy* (New York: New York University Press, 1969), p. 97. Interpolation mine.

"in terms of external observation," he not only abandons behaviorism as a substantive doctrine but also approaches Russell's conclusion that what can be retained of empiricism is only the condition that the verifiable consequences of the principles that constitute our knowledge "are such as experience will confirm."

Perhaps the most austere contemporary representative of the empiricist tradition is Nelson Goodman. In his very important analysis of inductive inference, he shows that the traditional empiricist approach left unresolved "the problem of differentiating between the regularities that do and those that do not . . . set the mind in motion," and suggests that we "regard the mind as in motion from the start, striking out with spontaneous predictions in dozens of directions, and gradually rectifying and channeling its predictive processes."[5] Like Hume, he appeals

> to past recurrences, but to recurrences in the explicit use of terms as well as to recurrent features of what is observed. Somewhat like Kant, we are saying that inductive validity depends not only upon what is presented but also upon how it is organized; but the organization we point to is effected by the use of language and is not attributed to anything inevitable or immutable in the nature of human cognition.

[5] Nelson Goodman, *Fact, Fiction and Forecast* (Cambridge, Mass.: Harvard University Press, 1955), pp. 89–90. Goodman adds that "we are not concerned with describing how the mind works but rather with describing or defining the distinction it makes between valid and invalid projections," but he occasionally discusses the "genetic problem" as well.

The "roots of inductive validity," he suggests, "are to be found in our use of language."[6]

But I think that Goodman rejects too quickly the objection that he is "trusting too blindly to a capricious Fate to see to it that just the right predicates get themselves comfortably entrenched," in the case of the "genetic problem." It is much too facile merely to say that "in the case of our main stock of well-worn predicates, I submit that the judgment of projectibility has derived from the habitual projection, rather than the habitual projection from the judgment of projectibility."[7] This suggestion fails entirely to explain the uniformities among individuals (or across species, even putting aside the problem of explaining induction in the absence of the explicit use of language). If the mind were, literally, to strike out at random from the start, there would be no reason to expect more than fortuitous similarities in judgment, even within the limited range of commonsense predicates that Goodman considers—terms denoting color, for example. In fact, Goodman seems to accept this consequence. Thus he seems to believe that whereas some speakers of English use the word "green" in the way that I assume everyone in the audience does, there are others who mean by "green" what we would mean by the (to us) complex predicate: examined before time t and green or examined after t and blue[8]

6 *Ibid.*, pp. 96, 117.

7 *Ibid.*, pp. 97–98.

8 Cf. Nelson Goodman, "The Emperor's New Ideas," in Hook, ed., *Language and Philosophy*, p. 140: "I am sure that speakers accustomed to projecting 'grue' rather than 'green' would be equally confident that animals use grue rather than green as a basis for generalization."

where *t*, say, might be midnight tonight. These unfortunates will be surprised, tomorrow, to discover that the things they look at and call "green" will match in color some of the things they examined yesterday and called "blue."[9] Goodman's conclusion has the merit of consistency. An austere empiricist, who believes that the mind is in motion from the start, striking out with spontaneous predictions without constraints, should reach this conclusion, along with many others that are equally bizarre. Goodman's analysis directly supports Russell's observation that either we know something independently of experience, or science is moonshine—as are the beliefs of common sense. His further speculations on how, given a system of hypotheses, one might proceed to adduce others, though interesting and suggestive, seem to me to leave quite untouched the central problems of acquisition of knowledge. It seems clear that if empiricism is to be taken seriously, it must be the "externalized empiricism" of Quine which "sees nothing uncongenial in the appeal to innate dispositions to overt behavior, innate readiness for language-learning," and requires only that "conjectures or conclusions . . . eventually be made sense of in terms of external observation."[10]

Recall that in his critique of Locke's *Essay Concerning Human Understanding,* Leibniz conjectured that by admitting reflection as a source of knowledge, Locke leaves the way open to reconstructing a rationalist theory in another terminology. Similarly, one might ask

[9] For a non-question-begging formulation, see my contribution to the same volume, pp. 71–72.

[10] "Linguistics and Philosophy," pp. 97–98.

to what extent even the "flavor" of empiricism is retained in a theory of acquisition of knowledge that
admits a quality space of unknown character, innate
structures of an arbitrary sort that permit the leap to
perhaps quite abstract hypotheses, principles of nondemonstrative inference that Leibniz might have called
the innate general principles that "enter into our
thoughts, of which they form the soul and the connection," principles that "can be discovered in us by dint
of attention, for which the senses furnish occasions, and
successful experience serves to confirm reason."

One might, in fact, reasonably go still further in
chipping away at traditional concepts of acquisition of
knowledge. Why should we suppose that the innate general principles, or the principles that integrate and
organize our mature systems of belief, should be dis-
coverable "by dint of attention"? It would seem to be
an empirical issue whether this is so (apart from ter-
minological debate about the concepts of "knowledge"
and "belief," debate that is likely to be fruitless, since
—as Russell observes—the concepts are unclear and
indeterminate). It is an open question, surely, whether
the "species of instinct" that determines "the experimental reasoning itself" does indeed "act in us unknown
to ourselves," as both Hume and Leibniz held, or perhaps even lies beyond introspection. It is, in fact, possible that insight into or understanding of these matters
lies beyond the scope of conscious human knowledge.
No contradiction follows from assuming this to be so,
though we may hope that it is not. The same innate
principles of mind that make possible the acquisition of
knowledge and systems of belief might also impose

limits on scientific understanding that exclude scientific knowledge of how knowledge and belief are acquired or used, though such understanding might be attainable by an organism differently or more richly endowed. It might be, in Kant's phrase, that the "schematism of our understanding, in its application to appearances and their mere form, is an art concealed in the depths of the human soul, whose real modes of activity nature is hardly likely ever to allow us to discover, and to have open to our gaze."[11] There is, surely, no reason for dogmatic assumptions on this score.

The notion that there may be innate principles of mind that on the one hand make possible the acquisition of knowledge and belief, and on the other, determine and limit its scope, suggests nothing that should surprise a biologist, so far as I can see. Writing on the specific case of postulated innate principles of language structure characteristic of the species, Jacques Monod observes:

> This conception has scandalized certain philosophers or anthropologists who see in it a return to Cartesian metaphysics. But if we accept its implicit biological content, this conception does not shock me at all.

It is quite reasonable to suppose that specific principles of language structure are a biological given, at the present stage of human evolution. Furthermore, Monod continues, it is likely that the evolution of human cortical structures was influenced by the early acquisition of

[11] Immanuel Kant, *A Critique of Pure Reason*, trans. Norman Kemp (New York: Random House, Modern Library, 1958), pp. 110–11.

a linguistic capacity, so that articulated language "not only has permitted the evolution of culture, but has contributed in a decisive fashion to the *physical* evolution of man"; and there is no paradox in supposing that "the linguistic capacity that reveals itself in the course of the epigenetic development of the brain is now a part of 'human nature,' " itself intimately associated with other aspects of cognitive function which may in fact have evolved in a specific way by virtue of the early use of articulated language.[12]

Having gone this far, one might well ask whether the residue of traditional empiricist speculation on the origin and growth of knowledge is not more of a hindrance than a help to a successful study of this problem. Consider, for example, the matter of "ostensive definition," which Russell, along with many others, takes to be a primitive or somehow basic stage in the acquisition of knowledge. A vocal noise, it is assumed, is associated with some notable feature of the environment and with an "idea" or "thought" of this feature. The word then "means" this feature in the sense that "its utterance can be caused by the feature in question, and the hearing of it can cause the 'idea' of this feature. This is the simplest kind of 'meaning,' out of which other kinds are developed." It is by reflection on such associations and similarities of stimuli "that the child, now become a philosopher, concludes that there is one word, 'mother,' and one person, Mother." "In time, by the use of Mill's canons, the infant, if he survives, will learn to speak correctly," identifying properly the relevant features of

[12] Jacques Monod, *Le Hasard et la nécessité* (Paris: Éditions du Seuil, 1970), pp. 150–51.

the environment and of the vocal expressions. It is such a process, Russell argues, that in theory leads to the belief in more or less permanent persons and things, the common-sense belief that makes so difficult any philosophy which dispenses with the notion of substance.[13] (Russell adds that he believes "this first step in philosophy to be mistaken," but that is another matter.) Quine suggests a somewhat similar process. For the infant, "mother, red, and water are . . . all of a type; each is just a history of sporadic encounter, a scattered portion of what goes on." The child "has mastered the scheme of enduring and recurring physical objects" only when he "has mastered the divided reference of general terms." After this he reassesses "Mama," retroactively, as a singular term, "the name of a broad and recurrent but withal individual object."[14]

The credibility of such speculations seems to me low, in the light of the little that is known. There is no reason at all to believe that the child's concept of enduring and recurring physical objects derives from his reflection on the use of language or on higher-level generalizations that are built on insights into language use, or that Mill's canons have anything to do with the interpretation of the world of experience in terms of permanent persons and things. Such slight experimental work as exists on this matter suggests that the concept of permanent and enduring objects is operative long before the use of language. Thus it appears that a child

[13] *Human Knowledge*, pp. 75–76.
[14] Willard V. O. Quine, *Word and Object* (Cambridge, Mass.: The M.I.T. Press, 1960), pp. 92–95.

only a few months old interprets the world in terms of perceptual constancies, and shows surprise if stimuli do not manifest the expected behavior of "enduring and recurring physical objects." If our conjectures are to be made sense of in terms of observation, it would seem that such observations support the conjecture that the "scheme of enduring and recurring individual objects" is primitive, rather than acquired in the course of language learning.

Much the same is true when we consider stimuli and their associated "ideas." Surveying some recent experimental work, Monod remarks that there can be no doubt that animals are capable of classifying objects and relations according to abstract categories, specifically geometric categories such as "triangle" and "circle"; to some extent experimental work has even identified the neural basis for such analysis. This work suggests that there is a primitive, neurologically given analytic system which may degenerate if not stimulated at an appropriate critical period, but which otherwise provides a specific interpretation of experience, varying with the organism to some extent. I think Monod is correct in commenting that "these modern discoveries thus give support, in a new sense, to Descartes and Kant, contrary to the radical empiricism that has dominated science for two centuries, throwing suspicion on any hypothesis that postulates the 'innateness' of forms of knowledge." So far as we know, animals learn according to a genetically determined program. There is no reason to doubt that this is also true of "the fundamental categories of human knowledge, and perhaps also other aspects of

human behavior, less fundamental, but of great significance for the individual and society."[15] In particular,
this may be true of man's apparently unique linguistic
faculties, and of his abilities of imaginative thought, as
manifested in language, in visual imagery, in plans of
action, or in true artistic or scientific creation.

A further residue of empiricist speculation appears
in Russell's analysis of proper names. He suggests, to
begin with, that "a proper name is a word designating
any continuous portion of space-time which sufficiently
interests us,"[16] but then adds that spatiotemporal continuity is not required. Again, it is an empirical problem
to determine what are the criteria for "nameability," not
by an arbitrary organism, or what Russell sometimes
calls a "logical saint," but by a biologically given human
mind. Spatiotemporal continuity is no doubt a factor, as
are certain figure-ground and other gestalt properties,
or the function of an object in a space of human action.
But the matter seems still more complex. For example, if
some physical arrangement of objects is created by an
artist as an example of a particular art form, it is nameable—say, a mobile, which need not meet the condition
of spatial continuity. But an arbitrary chance arrangement would not be considered a nameable "thing." If
this is correct, then our concept of "nameable thing"
involves a consideration of the intentions of the person
who produced the "thing." Further analysis would, no
doubt, show other, equally abstract conditions that
underlie the process of naming. It is difficult to imagine
that such conditions are learned, by Mill's canons or any

[15] Monod, *Le Hasard et la nécessité,* pp. 167–68.
[16] *Human Knowledge,* p. 89.

other scheme, though experience no doubt plays some role in refining the innately given schematism for interpretation of the world of human experience. The extent of its contribution is a matter to be determined by scientific investigation. But in this connection too, we should not be surprised if there is some truth to the dictum of the Cambridge Platonist Henry More that "the Soul sings out the whole Song upon the first hint, as knowing it very well before."

It has sometimes been argued that naming is ultimately inexplicable, and that the desire to explain naming beyond recording the facts of usage or providing "tests of the good construction of a series" is "the result of the Protean metaphysical urge to transcend language."[17] This seems an unnecessary conclusion. On the basis of evidence of usage and experimental tests, one can try to formulate a systematic theoretical account of the system of concepts that an individual has attained and puts to use, and further, to elaborate the a priori system of principles, conditions, and assumptions that led him to construct this system from his limited experience. It is difficult to see why such an enterprise, whatever its chances of success, reflects a "Protean metaphysical urge." It seems a fully intelligible program. Any theory of attained concepts or of the basis for the acquisition of a system of concepts will, to be sure, be underdetermined by evidence—the task is not a triviality. Furthermore, there is no antecedent reason to suppose that induction or "generalization," in any clear sense

[17] David Pears, "Universals," in Antony Flew, ed., *Logic and Language,* Second Series (New York: Philosophical Library, 1953), pp. 63, 64.

of these notions, will have much to do with the matter.

Russell assumes, with Wittgenstein and many others, that there are "two ways of getting to know what a word means": verbal definition, in terms of other words, or direct ostensive definition.[18] As a description of fact, this is dubious. True verbal definition is probably a very rare event. The difficulty of giving a verbal definition of ordinary concepts is well known. Consider the attempts, still surely only partially successful, to define such concepts as "game" or "promise," for example. What we generally call "verbal definitions" are mere hints, that can be interpreted properly by someone who already controls a rich, highly articulated theory of language and the world. But surely the same is true of "ostensive definition." Again, neither Mill's canons nor any other known scheme will account for the uniformity and specificity with which a child or an adult will understand what a new word means or denotes, under the conditions of ostensive definition. This will become quite obvious to anyone who attempts, say, to program a computer to do likewise. Under normal conditions we learn words by a limited exposure to their use. Somehow, our brief and personal and limited contacts with the world suffice for us to determine what words mean. When we try to analyze any specific instance—say, such readily learned words as "mistake," or "try," or "expect," or "compare," or "die," or even common nouns—we find that rather rich assumptions about the world of fact and the interconnections of concepts come into play in placing the item properly in the system of language. This is by now a familiar observation, and I need not elaborate

[18] *Human Knowledge,* p. 18.

on it. But it seems to me to further dissipate the lingering appeal of an approach to acquisition of knowledge that takes empiricist assumptions as a point of departure for what are presumed to be the simplest cases.

In fact, what substance is there to the claim that one part of empiricist theory appears to be true without any qualifications: namely, that words which I understand derive their meaning from my experience? That experience is required to bring innate structures into operation, to activate a system of innate ideas, is assumed quite explicitly, by Descartes, Leibniz, and others, as an integral part of theories that can hardly be regarded as "empiricist" if the term is to retain any significance. Beyond this, such differences as exist among individuals and across languages in the systems of concepts employed must be attributed to experience, if we assume, as seems reasonable, that there is no specific genetic adaptation to one or another language, and if we abstract away from individual variation in mental capacity. How extensive are these differences? An empirical question, obviously, but what little is known about the specificity and complexity of belief as compared with the poverty of experience leads one to suspect that it is at best misleading to claim that words that I understand derive their meaning from my experience.

Wittgenstein argued that "a word hasn't got a meaning given to it, as it were, by a power independent of us, so that there could be a kind of scientific investigation into what the word really means. A word has the meaning someone has given to it."[19] If the reference is to

[19] Ludwig Wittgenstein, *Blue and Brown Books* (Harper & Row, Harper Torchbooks, 1958), p. 28.

conscious, explicit explanations of meanings (or the readiness to give them, as Wittgenstein sometimes implies), the assertion can hardly be accepted. On the other hand, we can easily imagine how an organism initially endowed with conditions on the form and organization of language could construct a specific system of interconnections among concepts, and conditions of use and reference, on the basis of scanty evidence. There is no inherent mystery in this. For such an organism, we could certainly carry out a scientific investigation of these systematic structures and conditions, and it is unclear why this should not be described as part of a scientific investigation of what words really mean. Words would have the meaning given to them by the organism, to be sure, though there would be no necessity to suppose that this "giving of meaning" is conscious or accessible to introspection, or that the organism is at all capable of explaining the system of concepts it uses or describing the characteristics of particular items with any accuracy. In the case of humans, there is every reason to suppose that the semantic system of language is given largely by a power independent of conscious choice; the operative principles of mental organization are presumably inaccessible to introspection, but there is no reason why they should in principle be more immune to investigation than the principles that determine the physical arrangement of limbs and organs.

In trying to develop a "behavioral" analysis of linguistic expressions and their meanings, Russell considers the environmental causes of uttering an expression, the effects of hearing it, and the effects which the speaker expects or intends it to have on the hearer.[20] The latter consideration leads us to an investigation of reasons, as distinct from causes, and into the domain of "mental acts." I will not consider whether the analysis Russell presents is very convincing (I do not believe that it is), but here too he insists, quite correctly, that a study of stimuli and responses, or habit structures, will not get us very far. Though consideration of intended effects avoids some problems, it seems to me that no matter how fully elaborated, it will at best provide an analysis of successful communication, but not of meaning or of the use of language, which need not involve communication or even the attempt to communicate. If I use language to express or clarify my thoughts, with the intent to deceive, to avoid an embarrassing silence, or in a dozen other ways, my words have a strict meaning and I can very well mean what I say, but the fullest understanding of what I intend my audience (if any) to believe or to do might give little or no indication of the meaning of my discourse.

Russell suggests that the existence of "natural kinds" —a tendency for properties to cluster in limited varieties in the empirical world—facilitates common-sense inference, and that scientific knowledge is grounded in a series of principles that he develops in an interesting and detailed analysis. As an example, consider this principle:

> The physical world consists of units of a small number of different kinds, and there are causal laws governing the simpler structures that can be

[20] Bertrand Russell, *An Inquiry into Meaning and Truth* (London: George Allen & Unwin, 1940), p. 27 and elsewhere.

built out of such units, causing such structures to
fall into a rather small number of discretely differ-
ing kinds. There are also complexes of events
which act as causal units, being preceded and followed throughout some finite time by a series of
complexes of events all having approximately the
same structure and interrelated by spatiotemporal
contiguity.

The physical world, Russell writes, "has what might be
called 'habits', i.e., causal laws; the behaviour of animals has habits, partly innate, partly acquired," generated by "animal inference." "Owing to the world
being such as it is, certain kinds of inductions are justified and others are not." By reflection on such processes,
we arrive at canons of inference which "are valid if the
world has certain characteristics which we all believe it
to have."[21]

We might say, paraphrasing these remarks, that our
mental constitution permits us to arrive at knowledge
of the world insofar as our innate capacity to create
theories happens to match some aspect of the structure
of the world. By exploring various faculties of the mind,
we might, in principle, come to understand what theories
are more readily accessible to us than others, or what
potential theories are accessible to us at all, what forms
of scientific knowledge can be attained, if the world is
kind enough to have the required properties. Where
it is not, we may be able to develop a kind of "intellectual technology"—say, a technique of prediction that
will, for some reason, work within limits—but not to
attain what might properly be called scientific under-

[21] Russell, *Human Knowledge,* pp. 495–96.

standing or common-sense knowledge. Another organism, following different principles, might develop other sciences, or lack some of ours. Whether we will come to understand those aspects of human existence or physical reality, features of which intrigue us, we do not know, though the question might be answerable if we were to succeed in determining the principles of human understanding. It is this task that Russell's mature theory of knowledge presents to us, in an outline that is suggestive but, as he insists, no more than that.

To pursue this task, we must investigate specific domains of human knowledge or systems of belief, determine their character, and study their relation to the brief and personal experience on which they are erected. A system of knowledge and belief results from the interplay of innate mechanisms, genetically determined maturational processes, and interaction with the social and physical environment. The problem is to account for the system constructed by the mind in the course of this interaction. The particular system of human knowledge that has, so far, lent itself most readily to such an approach is the system of human language. In the study of language we need not (to a first approximation, at least) make the distinction between knowledge and belief. There is no objective external standard against which to check the system of rules and principles relating sound and meaning—the grammar—constructed by the mind. By definition, a person knows his language (or several dialects and languages) perfectly, though we can ask how the system created by one speaker matches that of another. It seems to make little sense to say that a mature speaker does not know his own dialect, say, of English; though it might be that there are idiosyncratic features that distinguish his grammar from that of the speech communities in which he lives. At least, this is true to the extent—not inconsiderable—that we can divorce the study of language and its structure from questions of empirical belief and knowledge of fact. In one sense, a person's knowledge of language reflects his capacity to acquire knowledge in a relatively "pure form." One might argue, for this reason, that this is not a "central case" of human knowledge, and perhaps not an illuminating case.[22] It seems to me that caution is in order. We can raise seriously the question of acquisition of knowledge only where we have a reasonably convincing characterization of what has been learned. We lack any such characterization in the case of standard examples of common-sense knowledge or belief: for example, with regard to the behavior of physical objects, or human social behavior, or the relations of action and motives, and so on.

Some have argued rather differently, proposing that acquisition of language is based on more general principles that underlie other forms of learning as well. Such views will gain substance to the extent that their proponents can show how specific aspects of knowledge of language—some of which I will discuss in a moment —can be explained in terms of more general "learning strategies" or "principles of development." Since only the vaguest of suggestions have been offered, it is impossible, at present, to evaluate these proposals.

[22] See Roy Edgely, "Innate Ideas," in G. N. A. Vesey, ed., *Knowledge and Necessity,* Royal Institute of Philosophy Lectures (New York: St. Martin's Press, 1970), for an interesting discussion of this matter.

Knowledge of language results from the interplay of initially given structures of mind, maturational processes, and interaction with the environment. Thus there is no reason to expect that there will be invariant properties of the knowledge that is acquired—the grammars constructed by the mind—even if the innate determination of initial structures and maturational processes is quite restrictive. Suppose, however, that we discover certain invariant properties of human language. In such a case it is always a plausible (though not necessarily correct) hypothesis that these invariants reflect properties of mind, just as, if we were to discover invariant properties of the song of some species of bird, it would be plausible to suggest that these are genetically determined. This is an empirical hypothesis, falsifiable by factual evidence. The alternative to it would be the hypothesis that the invariants in question result from certain well-defined "learning strategies" applied to a sufficiently uniform environment. In the cases I will discuss, and many others, this alternative seems to me most implausible. In any case, the empirical conditions of the investigation are clear.

Invariance can appear at several levels of abstraction and significance. For example, in investigating a particular dialect of English, we discover similarities of usage among speakers of varying personal experience. Furthermore, investigation of a wide range of languages reveals invariant properties that are by no means necessary for a system of thought and communication. For example, it is conceivable that the principle of "nameability" in some language might be the simple condition that Russell investigates: that a continuous portion of space-time is a possible "nameable thing." But in human languages, it seems that other conditions enter into determining what are "nameable" things, as noted earlier. As we investigate other aspects of the representation of meaning, additional properties of language come to light. Consider the meaning of sentences. Some aspects of sentence meaning are determined by the ordering of words and their arrangement into phrases, while others are related to structures of a much more abstract sort. To take a simple case, consider the sentences "John appealed to Bill to like himself" and "John appeared to Bill to like himself."[23] The two sentences are virtually identical in surface form, but obviously quite different in interpretation. Thus when I say "John appealed to Bill to like himself," I mean that Bill is to like himself; but when I say "John appeared to Bill to like himself," it is John who likes himself. It is only at what I would call the level of "deep structure" that the semantically significant grammatical relations are directly expressed in this case.

The example illustrates relations of meaning among words, but semantic representation involves relations among phrases as well. Suppose I say, "I would speak about such matters with enthusiasm." The statement is ambiguous: it may mean that my speaking would be enthusiastic, or that I would be pleased to speak about such matters. The phrase "with enthusiasm" is associated either with the verb "speak" or with the phrase "speak about such matters." Investigating questions of

[23] The example is due to R. Dougherty. In subsequent discussion, I will borrow freely, without further specific attribution, from the work of Joan Bresnan, Howard Lasnik, Michael Helke, Paul Postal, and others.

this nature, we can, I believe, develop some reasonable though still only partial and tentative hypotheses as to how the meaning of sentences must be represented in human language, and how such representations relate to various aspects of linguistic form: order, phrasing, and abstract structures that relate in no simple way to the physical utterance.

Turning to the physical aspect of language, we reach similar conclusions. There are many imaginable physical dimensions that might, in principle, be used to determine the sounds of speech, but in fact the variety of human languages makes use of only a restricted range of properties. Furthermore, as the study of language has revealed since Ferdinand de Saussure's pioneering work, the sounds of language enter into systematic relations in accordance with restrictive principles. More remarkable still is the fact that the systematic structure of sound patterns is revealed most strikingly when we consider, not the sounds themselves in their physical aspect, but rather an abstract sound pattern that is mapped into a physical representation by ordered rules of a narrowly constrained type, rules which, applying in sequence, convert an abstract underlying representation of sound into a physical structure that may not bear a close point-by-point resemblance to the underlying mental representation. It is in this domain, in my opinion, that recent studies of language have obtained some of their most important insights.[24]

[24] See Noam Chomsky and Morris Halle, *Sound Patterns of English* (New York: Harper & Row, 1968), for a presentation of a general theory of sound structure applied to English. See also the more recent work of Steven Anderson, Michael Brame, Joan Bresnan, Charles Kisseberth, and others.

By studying the representation of sound and the representation of meaning in natural language, we can obtain some understanding of invariant properties that might reasonably be attributed to the organism itself as its contribution to the task of acquisition of knowledge, the schematism that it applies to the data of sense in its effort to organize experience and construct cognitive systems. But some of the most interesting and surprising results concern rather the system of rules that relate sound and meaning in natural language. These rules fall into various categories and exhibit invariant properties that are by no means necessary for a system of thought or communication, a fact that once again has intriguing implications for the study of human intelligence.

Consider, for example, the way in which questions are formed in English. Consider the sentence "The dog in the corner is hungry." From this, we can form the question "Is the dog in the corner hungry?" by a simple formal operation: moving the element "is" to the front of the sentence. Given a variety of examples of question formation, a linguist studying English might propose several possible rules of question formation. Imagine two such proposals. The first states that to form a question, we first identify the subject noun phrase of the sentence, and we then move the occurrence of "is" following this noun phrase to the beginning of the sentence. Thus in the example in question, the subject noun phrase is "the dog in the corner"; we form the question by moving the occurrence of "is" that follows it to the front of the sentence. Let us call this operation a "structure-dependent operation," meaning by this that the operation considers not merely the sequence of elements that constitute the sentence but also their structure; in this case, the fact that the sequence "the dog in the corner" is a phrase, furthermore a noun phrase. For the case in question, we might also have proposed a "structure-independent operation": namely, take the leftmost occurrence of "is" and move it to the front of the sentence. We can easily determine that the correct rule is the structure-dependent operation. Thus if we have the sentence "The dog that is in the corner is hungry," we do not apply the proposed structure-independent operation, forming the question "Is the dog that ———— in the corner is hungry?" Rather, we apply the structure-dependent operation, first locating the noun-phrase subject "the dog that is in the corner," then inverting the occurrence of "is" that follows it, forming: "Is the dog that is in the corner ———— hungry?"

Though the example is trivial, the result is nonetheless surprising, from a certain point of view. Notice that the structure-dependent operation has no advantages from the point of view of communicative efficiency or "simplicity." If we were, let us say, designing a language for formal manipulations by a computer, we would certainly prefer structure-independent operations. These are far simpler to carry out, since it is only necessary to scan the words of the sentence, paying no attention to the structures into which they enter, structures that are not marked physically in the sentence at all. Mathematicians have studied structure-independent operations on strings (inversion, shuffling, etc.), but it has occurred to no one to investigate the curious and complex notion of "structure-dependent operation," in the relevant sense. Notice further that we have very little evidence, in our normal experience, that the structure-dependent operation is the correct one. It is quite possible for a person to go through life without having heard any relevant examples that would choose between the two principles. It is, however, safe to predict that a child who has had no such evidence would unerringly apply the structure-dependent operation the first time he attempts to form the question corresponding to the assertion "The dog that is in the corner is hungry." Though children make certain kinds of errors in the course of language learning, I am sure that none make the error of forming the question "Is the dog that in the corner is hungry?" despite the slim evidence of experience and the simplicity of the structure-independent rule. Furthermore, all known formal operations in the grammar of English, or of any other language, are structure-dependent. This is a very simple example of an invariant principle of language, what might be called a formal linguistic universal or a principle of universal grammar.

Given such facts, it is natural to postulate that the idea of structure-dependent operations is part of the innate schematism applied by the mind to the data of experience. The idea is "innate to the mind" in the sense in which Descartes argued that "the idea of a true triangle" is innate: "because we already possess within us the idea of a true triangle, and it can be more easily conceived by our mind than the more complex figure of the triangle drawn on paper, we, therefore, when we see that composite figure, apprehend not it itself, but rather the authentic triangle."[25] As noted earlier, there

[25] *The Philosophical Works of Descartes,* trans. E. S. Haldane and G. R. T. Ross (New York: Dover Publications, 1955),

are now the glimmerings of understanding of the neuro-
physiological structures that provide such schemata for
interpretation of experience in the case of figures and
objects, though the neurophysiology of language remains
almost a total mystery. It does seem quite reasonable to
propose, however, that the unknown structures of the
brain that provide knowledge of language on the basis
of the limited data available to us "possess within themselves" the idea of structure-dependent operations.

Studying language more carefully, we find many
other examples of quite remarkable properties that appear to be inexplicable on the basis of experience alone.
To take another simple case, consider the sentence "I
believe the dog to be hungry." There is a corresponding
passive: "The dog is believed to be hungry." We might
propose, as a first approximation, that the passive is
formed by the structure-dependent operation that locates
the main verb and the noun phrase that follows it,
inverting the two, and adding various modifications that
need not concern us.

Consider next the sentence "I believe the dog's
owner to be hungry." Applying the postulated operation,
we locate the main verb "believe" and the noun phrase

Vol. 2, pp. 227–28. For further discussion and references, see
my *Cartesian Linguistics* (New York: Harper & Row, 1966);
Aspects of the Theory of Syntax (Cambridge, Mass.: The M.I.T.
Press, 1965), Chap. 1; and *Language and Mind* (New York:
Harcourt Brace Jovanovich, 1968). On English precursors of
Kant in the study of the "conformity of objects to our mode of
cognition" and "rationalistic idealism" more generally, see
Arthur Lovejoy, "Kant and the English Platonists," *Essays
Philosophical and Psychological: In Honor of William James*
(New York: Longmans, Green & Company, 1908).

"the dog" following it, as before, and form "The dog is believed 's owner to be hungry." Obviously, this is incorrect. What we must do is choose not the noun phrase "the dog," but rather the noun phrase of which it is a part, "the dog's owner," giving then: "The dog's owner is believed to be hungry." The instruction for forming passives was ambiguous: the ambiguity is resolved by the overriding principle that we must apply the operation to the largest noun phrase that immediately follows the verb. This, again, is a rather general property of the formal operations of syntax. There has been some fairly intensive investigation of such conditions on formal operations in the past decade, and although we are far from a definitive formulation, some interesting things have been learned. It seems reasonably clear that these conditions must also be part of the schematism applied by the mind in language-learning. Again, the conditions seem to be invariant, insofar as they are understood at all, and there is little data available to the language-learner to show that they apply.

An interesting property of the formal operations of language is that though they are structure-dependent, they are, in an important sense, independent of meaning. Compare the sentences "I believed your testimony," "I believed your testimony to be false," and "I believed your testimony to have been given under duress." The corresponding passives are "Your testimony was believed," "Your testimony was believed to be false," and "Your testimony was believed to have been given under duress." In all cases, the passive is formed by the rule informally described a moment ago. The rule pays no

attention to the grammatical and semantic relations of
the main verb to the noun phrase that follows it. Thus in
"I believed your testimony," the noun phrase is the grammatical object of "believe." In "I believed your testimony to be false," it bears no relation to "believe," and
is the subject of "be false." In "I believed your testimony to have been given under duress," it bears no
relation to "believe" and is the grammatical object of
the embedded verb "give." Yet in all cases, the rule
applies blindly, caring nothing for these differences.[26]
Thus in an important sense, the rules are structure-
dependent and only structure-dependent. Technically,
they are rules that apply to abstract labeled bracketing
of sentences (abstract, in that it is not physically indi-
cated), not to systems of grammatical or semantic relations. Again, there is no a priori necessity for this to be
true. These characteristics of language, if true, are empirical facts. It is reasonable to suppose that they are
"a priori" for the organism, in that they define, for him,
what counts as a human language, and determine the
general character of his acquired knowledge of language.
But it is easy to imagine systems of language that would
depart from these principles. If our hypotheses are cor-

[26] It might be argued that the latter two sentences derive,
not by passivization, but by *"it-replacement"* from "it is believed
[your testimony . . .]." If so, the same comments apply to this
rule and the others involved in the derivation. It should be
noted that lexical properties of particular items determine the
permissibility of transformations and that rules of semantic interpretation may be inapplicable in certain cases if transformations have applied. This "filtering effect" of transformations in
effect makes them inapplicable in certain cases.

rect, such systems should be impossible for human children to learn in the normal way, though perhaps they might be learned as a kind of puzzle or intellectual exercise.

I might mention at this point that this account is extremely misleading in that I have spoken of formal operations on sentences. In fact, the careful study of language shows that these operations apply to abstract forms underlying sentences, to structures that may be quite remote from the actual physical events that constitute spoken or written language. (As noted earlier, the same is true in the case of sound structure.) These structures and the operations that apply to them are postulated as mental entities in our effort to understand what one has learned, when he has come to know a human language, and to explain how sentences are formed and understood. I would like to emphasize that there is nothing strange or occult in this move, any more than in the postulation of genes or electrons. For simplicity of exposition, I will continue to use the misleading notion of "operations on sentences," but the oversimplification should be borne in mind.

The account is misleading in another respect as well. The rules in question are not laws of nature, nor, of course, are they legislated or laid down by any authority. They are, if our theorizing is correct, rules that are constructed by the mind in the course of acquisition of knowledge. They can be violated, and in fact, departure from the rules can often be an effective literary device. To take a particularly simple example, Rebecca West, in criticism of the view that art reflects nature, wrote: "A copy of the universe is not what is required of art;

one of the damned thing is ample."[27] The statement violates the rule of grammar that requires a plural noun in such phrases as "one of the books is here" or "one of the damned things is enough." But the statement is nevertheless exactly to the point. We can often exploit the expressive resources of language most fully by departing from its principles. The "degree of logical or grammatical disorder" is one of William Empson's dimensions of ambiguity: deviation from strict grammatical rule is one device to force the reader to "invent a variety of reasons and order them in his own mind" in seeking to determine the meaning of what is said— "the essential fact about the poetical use of language," Empson suggests, but a feature of normal usage as well, for similar reasons.[28] This too should be borne in mind when I speak loosely about what can and cannot be said, grammatically.

The examples I have mentioned so far have been discussed in recent literature.[29] To illustrate further, I would like to turn to some still unexplored territory. I mentioned a moment ago that we form passives by inverting the main verb of a sentence and the noun phrase that follows it. Sometimes, however, the opera-

[27] Cited by M. H. Abrams in *The Mirror and the Lamp: Romantic Theory and the Critical Tradition* (New York: Oxford University Press, 1953), p. 100.

[28] William Empson, *Seven Types of Ambiguity* (New York: New Directions Pub. Corp., 1947), pp. 48. 25.

[29] For a more careful discussion of the topics that follow and related questions, see my "Conditions on Transformations," to appear in Steven Anderson and R. P. V. Kiparsky, eds., *Studies Presented to Morris Halle* (New York: Holt, Rinehart & Winston, forthcoming).

tion is impermissible. Consider the sentence "I believe the dog is hungry." We cannot form "The dog is believed is hungry," though from the sentence "I believe the dog to be hungry" we can form "The dog is believed to be hungry." How can we account for this difference? It might, of course, be that this is simply an idiosyncrasy of English, learned by experience. Let us explore the more interesting possibility that this is not so, and ask what kinds of principles might account for such a difference.

To begin with, notice that the two sentences in question ("I believe the dog is hungry," "I believe the dog to be hungry") consist of the subject "I," the main verb "believe," and an embedded structure of the form of a sentence: "the dog is hungry," "the dog to be hungry." Let us distinguish two types of embedded sentences: tensed sentences such as "the dog is hungry" and non-tensed sentences such as "the dog to be hungry." Only the former, of course, can appear as a nonembedded sentence. As a first guess, let us propose the principles that nothing can be extracted from a tensed sentence.

Other examples suggest that this principle can be generalized. Consider the sentence "The candidates each hated the other." A variant is "The candidates hated each other." There are persuasive arguments, which I will not review here, that the latter is formed from the former by a rule that moves the word "each" over the main verb, replacing the word "the" of the object phrase "the other." Consider next the sentence "The candidates each expected the other to win." Applying the rule, we can form "The candidates expected each other to win."

Consider next the sentence "The candidates each expected that the other would win" or "The candidates each believed the other would win." We cannot apply the rule, in either case, to form "The candidates expected that each other would win" or "The candidates believed each other would win." To account for this difference, let us generalize our earlier principle and propose that nothing can be extracted from or introduced into an embedded tensed sentence. More generally, let us propose that no rule can involve the phrase X and the phrase Y, where Y is contained in a tensed sentence to the right of X: i.e., no rule can involve X and Y in the structure [...X...[...Y...]...], where [...Y...] is a tensed sentence.

Before investigating some apparent counterexamples to this principle, let us consider some cases that suggest still another condition relating embedded structures and phrases outside them. Consider the sentence "John expected to win." It has generally been assumed, in modern studies of English grammar, that this derives from an underlying structure containing an embedded sentence of the form: noun phrase—win, where a rule assigns an anaphoric relation, a relation of coreference in this case, to the noun phrase and the subject of the full sentence. The embedded noun phrase is then deleted. Thus if grammatical relations are assigned prior to deletion, it will follow that "John" will be understood to be the subject of "win" as well as of "expect" in "John expected to win," as is of course the case. There are syntactic reasons for this assumption, which I will not review. Let us accept it, then, taking the noun phrase of the embedded sentence to be a pronoun which is deleted after being assigned an anaphoric relation to its antecedent.

Consider next the sentence "The candidates each expected to defeat the other." By our assumption, this derives from the underlying form "The candidates each expected [pronoun—to defeat the other]," where brackets enclose the embedded nontensed sentence. By the rule of *each*-movement, followed by deletion of the pronoun, we derive "The candidates expected to defeat each other," in conformity with the facts.

Consider next the sentence "The men each expected the soldier to shoot the other." The rule of *each*-movement should apply, as in the preceding case, giving "The men expected the soldier to shoot each other." Obviously, this is incorrect. Some condition prevents movement of "each" into the embedded nontensed sentence in this case.

The principle that suggests itself at once is this: Where the embedded sentence contains a full subject, no rule can involve an item X to the left of this sentence and an item Y in its predicate. More formally, no rule can involve X and Y in the structure: ... X ... [Z — ... Y ...], where Z is the lexically specified subject of ... Y .... Loosely put, no rule can relate items across the subject of an embedded phrase. This principle is supported by many other examples. Consider the sentence "The candidates each heard denunciations of the other." The grammatical object of "heard" is the complex noun phrase "denunciations of the other." The principle of *each*-movement applies, giving "The candidates heard denunciations of each other." But suppose that this complex noun phrase contains a subject, as in "The candidates each heard John's denunciations of the

other," where "John" is the subject of "denunciation."[30]
We cannot, in this case, apply *each*-movement to give
"The candidates heard John's denunciations of each
other." The latter, though of course intelligible, is jar-
ring to the ear in a way in which "The candidates heard
denunciations of each other" is not. The suggested principle explains the distinction. Notice that in this case,
the principle applies not to an embedded sentence but
to an embedded complex noun phrase with the form of
a sentence. The same distinction appears in the pair
"The men saw pictures of each other," "The men saw
John's pictures of each other." The same is true of many
other cases.

These examples illustrate one case of the suggested
principle: namely, that a general constraint blocks inser-
tion of an item under the specified conditions. Similarly,
extraction of an item is blocked under the same conditions. Consider the sentence "You saw pictures of
someone." In colloquial English, we can form the corresponding question "Who did you see pictures of?"
But the question "Who did you see John's pictures of?"
from "You saw John's pictures of someone" is far less

---

[30] Use of the term "subject" requires explanation. For an
appropriate definition and an explanation of why it is proper to
regard "John" as the "subject" of "denounce," "denunciation,"
"picture," in "John denounced Bill," "John's denunciation of
Bill," "John's picture of Bill," respectively, see my "Remarks on
Nominalization," in R. A. Jacobs and P. S. Rosenbaum, eds.,
Readings in English Transformational Grammar (Boston: Ginn
& Company, 1970). The careful reader will notice that I am
using the term "subject of" with a slight ambiguity. Thus in
"John denounces Bill," I refer to "John" as the subject of
"denounces" and also as the subject of "denounces Bill." Sim-
ilarly, in "John's denunciation of Bill."

natural, because of the cited principle. Again, there are similar cases with other constructions.

Consider a rule of a very different sort. It has been observed that such sentences as "I saw us" or "We saw me" are strange, as compared with "They saw us" or "I saw them." Suppose, then, that some rule of interpretation assigns the property "strangeness" to a sentence of the form: noun phrase—verb—noun phrase—X, where the two noun phrases intersect in reference. This is, no doubt, a special case of a more general principle of interpretation that leads us to try to assign difference of reference to noun phrases under a variety of formal conditions. Thus if I say "The soldiers detested the officers," you would naturally understand me as referring to a set of soldiers disjoint from the set of officers, though there is no semantic absurdity in considering the two sets to overlap—e.g., if the soldiers hated the officers among them, perhaps even themselves. In the case of the first-person pronouns, it is impossible to assign disjoint reference; hence the strangeness of the sentences.

But now consider the two sentences "I expected them to hate us" and "I expected us to hate them." Clearly the second, but not the first, has the property of strangeness of "I saw us." The principle in question explains the difference. The rule of interpretation does not apply, assigning strangeness, when the two personal pronouns "I" and "us" are separated by the subject of the embedded sentence.

Finally, let us turn to a somewhat more complex example. Consider the sentence "I didn't see many of the pictures." In colloquial usage, this would normally be interpreted as meaning "I saw few of the pictures," i.e., not many of the pictures are such that I saw them. There is a secondary interpretation, namely: Many of the pictures are such that I didn't see them. Under the latter interpretation, I could truly say "I didn't see many of the pictures" if there were a hundred pictures and I had seen just fifty. Thus I didn't see fifty, but I did see fifty others. Under the former and, I believe, more normal interpretation, I could not truly say "I didn't see many of the pictures" under these conditions, though I could truly say it if I had seen just three of the hundred pictures.

Consider next the sentence "I didn't see pictures of many of the children." Again, there are two interpretations. Under what I am calling the "normal" interpretation, it means that I saw pictures of few of the children. Under the secondary interpretation, it means "Pictures of many of the children are such that I didn't see them" (although perhaps I did see pictures of many of the children as well).

The "normal" interpretation in both cases associates "not" with "many." The secondary interpretation associates "not" with the main verb "see."

Consider next the sentence "I didn't see John's pictures of many of the children." Here, I believe, the "normal" interpretation is ruled out. The sentence cannot, without extreme artificiality, be interpreted as meaning "I saw John's pictures of (only) few of the children." For speakers who find the secondary interpretation unacceptable in the earlier cases, there will be no natural interpretation of this sentence. Other speakers, I believe, will interpret it naturally as meaning only

"John's pictures of many of the children are such that I didn't see them" (though perhaps I did see John's pictures of many of the children). Though the examples are moderately subtle, I think that this statement of the facts is correct. If so, notice that it follows from the principle in question. Association of "not" with "many" is blocked by the principle that items cannot be related when separated by the subject of an embedded sentence.

Notice some interesting properties of the principles in question. First, they are extremely general, applying to formal operations that modify the form of sentences as well as rules of interpretation of sentences. Second, they appear to have no obvious motivation on the basis of semantic or other considerations of communicative utility. Correspondingly, violation of the principles often gives intelligible though somewhat odd-sounding forms. These characteristics are typical of many of the general conditions that have been tentatively proposed as linguistic universals, formal invariants of language.

Let us turn briefly to some apparent violations of the principles. Consider the sentence "Did you tell me that Bill was there?" Correspondingly, we can form the question "Where did you tell me that Bill was?" This operation violates both of the conditions I have proposed. The question-word "where" is extracted from the embedded tensed sentence "Bill was there" and furthermore, it is moved over the subject of this sentence. How can we account for these violations, for the difference between this operation and the others that we have discussed?

There is strong evidence that the underlying form of sentences consists not merely of a subject and a predicate, but of the structure: complementizer—subject—predicate, where the complementizer can be null in the output, but can also be realized as such items as "that," "for," and question-words, as in *"That the dog was hungry* surprised me," *"For the dog to be hungry* is odd," *"What the dog ate* is unknown," and so on. Let us propose that to form questions, the question-words move into the complementizer position. Let us now modify our principles to permit an item to escape from a tensed sentence if and only if it is in the complementizer position. I will also invoke here another well-confirmed principle, namely, that operations apply in a cyclic fashion, first to the most deeply embedded structures, then to the structures that contain them, and so on.

Consider now our problem sentence "Where did you tell me that Bill was?" The underlying structure is: complementizer—you tell me [complementizer—Bill—was somewhere]. In the first cycle, we form "where" from "somewhere" and move the question-word to the embedded complementizer position, violating no principles. This yields: complementizer—you tell me [where Bill was]. In the second cycle, we reapply the rule, moving "where" to the complementizer position of the main sentence, as is now permitted by the modification of the principles. This gives "Where did you tell me (that) Bill was?"[31] Depending on semantic properties of the main verb, the rule may or may not apply on the second cycle. If it does not, we derive such sentences as "I wonder where Bill was."

These proposals have several empirical conse-

[31] I omit here some technical details, e.g., the rules that spell out the complementizer position optionally as "that."

quences. I will not trace the reasoning in detail, but the reader can determine for himself that they block such sentences as "Where do you wonder whom Bill saw?" from the abstract form "You wonder [Bill saw someone somewhere.]" The same considerations block "Whom do you wonder whether Bill saw" or "What does Bill know how we do?" though they will permit "Whom do you think (that) Bill saw?" or "What does Bill know how to do?" for example. These principles predict that an item will be able to escape from an embedded sentence in apparent violation of the principles just in case there is, on independent grounds, a rule that moves the item to the complementizer position of the sentence. Thus question-words can escape, but escape is impossible from the complex noun phrase "John's picture of Bill," since noun phrases contain no complementizer (thus "Whom did you see John's picture of?" is blocked). Similarly, escape is impossible in the case of passivization applied to "I believe John was here" (blocking "John is believed is here"), since there is no independent rule moving the subject of the embedded sentence to the complementizer position.

Space limits prevent further discussion, but it is not difficult to show that if these principles are carefully formulated, they will also account for many other well-known distinctions: for example, the distinction between "Whom do you believe that John saw?" (from "You believe that John saw someone") and the impossible "Whom do you believe the claim that John saw?" (from "You believe the claim that John saw someone"). The result follows from careful definition of the principle of cyclic application: the rule forming questions applies to adjacent structures, that is, one structure and another in which the first is directly embedded. A number of other interesting consequences follow, if we pursue the matter further.

The major point that I want to show, by this brief and informal discussion, is that there apparently are deep-seated and rather abstract principles of a very general nature that determine the form and interpretation of sentences. It is reasonable to formulate the empirical hypothesis that such principles are language universals. Quite probably the hypothesis will have to be qualified as research into the variety of languages continues. To the extent that such hypotheses are tenable, it is plausible to attribute the proposed language invariants to the innate language faculty which is, in turn, one component of the structure of mind. These are, I stress, empirical hypotheses. Alternatives are conceivable. For example, one might argue that children are specifically trained to follow the principles in question, or, more plausibly, that these principles are special cases of more general principles of mind. As already noted, it is impossible to evaluate such suggestions until they are given some reasonable formulation.

I have stressed throughout that in the cases discussed there appears to be no general explanation for the observed phenomena in terms of communicative efficiency or "simplicity." In other words, there seems to be no "functional explanation" for the observations in question. In some cases the principles may serve to reduce ambiguity, but at most marginally. One can easily imagine systems of communication or expression of thought that have structure-independent operations,

operations on networks of semantic relations, operations that violate the formal principles suggested, or conditions that would eliminate the possibility of such ambiguities as we find commonly in natural language (e.g., consider "She is too old-fashioned to marry," where "she" may be interpreted as subject or object of "marry"; it is easy to imagine conditions that would eliminate such ambiguities, but they do not operate, so far as is known, in natural languages). There is no particular reason, so far as I can see, why a language used for the purposes of natural language could not depart from the formal principles discussed and proposed here. This fact, if fact it is, is important. A traditional view holds that language is "a mirror of mind." This is true, in some interesting sense, insofar as properties of language are "species-specific"—not explicable on some general grounds of functional utility or simplicity that would apply to arbitrary systems that serve the purposes of language. Where properties of language can be explained on such "functional" grounds, they provide no revealing insight into the nature of mind. Precisely because the explanations proposed here are "formal explanations," precisely because the proposed principles are not essential or even natural properties of any imaginable language, they provide a revealing mirror of mind (if correct). Such principles, we may speculate, are a priori for the species—they provide the framework for the interpretation of experience and the construction of specific forms of knowledge on the basis of experience—but are not necessary or even natural properties of all imaginable systems that might serve the functions of human language. It is for this reason that these principles are of interest for the study of the nature of the human mind.

In contrast, consider the fact that sentences are not likely to exceed a certain length. There is no difficulty in suggesting a "functional explanation" for this fact; for exactly this reason, it is of no interest for the study of mind. It is quite legitimate, evidently, to abstract away from this property of language use in our effort to understand the nature of human language. Or consider the observation known as "Zipf's law":[32] namely, if the words of a long text are ranked in order of frequency, we discover that frequency is expressible as a function of rank in accordance with a fixed "law" (with a few parameters), which I need not elaborate here. As Benoit Mandelbrot proved, the same is true of texts produced by a vast range of imaginable processes. Specifically, if we have a finite source that produces symbols in sequence (under a wide range of statistical conditions) and we designate one of these symbols as "space," defining "words" as sequences of symbols between successive occurrences of space, then these "words" will obey Zipf's law in their rank-frequency distribution. If, say, we take an English text and take the letter e to be space, defining "words" as sequences bounded by successive occurrences of the letter e, then these words will obey Zipf's law. Thus the fact that actual words come

---

[32] See George K. Zipf, *The Psycho-Biology of Language: An Introduction to Dynamic Philology* (Cambridge, Mass.: The M.I.T. Press, 1965 [1st ed. Boston: Houghton Mifflin Company, 1935]). For discussion, see G. A. Miller and Noam Chomsky, "Finitary Models of Language Users," in Robert D. Luce, Robert R. Bush, and Eugene Galanter, eds., *Handbook of Mathematical Psychology* (New York: John Wiley & Sons, 1963), Vol. 2.

fairly close to this predicted distribution is of virtually no interest. It is a fact that can be explained on quite general grounds, in terms of assumptions that could hardly fail to be true. Or consider a third case. It has been observed that hearers have great difficulty in interpreting sentences in which a relative clause is completely embedded within another relative clause: for example, the sentence "The book that the man read is interesting" is readily interpretable, but the sentence "The book that the man the girl married read is interesting" is much less so. This observation is easily explained on the assumption that in processing a sentence, a hearer applies a "relative-clause-analysis procedure," and that it is difficult to call upon a given analytic procedure in the course of applying that very procedure (returning again to the original application after the internal application is completed). This is a natural principle for a wide range of temporal processing systems, and insofar as it accounts for the difficulty of interpreting so-called "self-embedded" constructions, the result is of little interest. I do not want to overstate the point, or to suggest that there is a precise boundary between two types of explanation and principle, but in a general way it is correct, I believe, to say that "formal explanations" based on properties of language that are by no means essential or even natural for arbitrary systems with the functions of natural language are particularly significant for the study of language as a mirror of mind. It is quite striking that despite considerable effort, few plausible examples have been suggested of "functional explanations" of general linguistic phenomena; and where they have been plausibly proposed, it seems that they are not expressible in the framework of formal grammar—a conclusion that reinforces the belief that the principles of formal grammar do express the properties of a basic component of the human mind, not directly observed, of course, but subject to investigation under an idealization that is quite legitimate.

This discussion barely touches on a few of the areas where linguistic invariants have been tentatively, but I think rather plausibly, identified. A natural further step would be to investigate the principles of language use. Here too, interesting ideas have been explored. I see no reason why other domains of human intelligence might not be amenable to such investigation. Perhaps, in this way, we can characterize the structure of various systems of human knowledge and belief, various systems of performance and interaction. Insofar as such efforts are successful, it is possible to pose in a serious way the central problem of what might reasonably be called "learning theory," namely, Russell's question: "how comes it that human beings, whose contacts with the world are brief and personal and limited, are nevertheless able to know as much as they do know?" I believe that the study of human psychology has been diverted into side channels by an unwillingness to pose the problem of how experience is related to knowledge and belief, a problem which of course presupposes a logically (though not necessarily temporally) prior investigation of the structure of systems of knowledge and belief. No matter how successfully the study of stimulus-response connections, habit structures, and so on is pursued, it will always fail to touch these central questions. The systems of knowledge and belief that underlie normal human behavior simply cannot be described in terms of networks of association, fabrics of dispositions to respond, habit structures, and the like. At least, this seems to be true in the case of language and other known examples of human "cognitive processes."

With regard to the specificity of the language faculty, there is little to say, at the moment. Nothing is known that bears much similarity to the principles discovered in the course of the study of language—for example, those I have mentioned. Perhaps this means that the innate schematism that the child brings to bear in language learning is unique to language. If so, the neurologist faces the problem of discovering the mechanisms that determine this schematism, and the biologist, the problem of explaining how these developed in the course of human evolution. If, on the contrary, we discover that other skills and competences involve the same or related schemata, the result is again interesting, and poses the same challenges. Many regard the former conclusion as most implausible. It is difficult to see the grounds for this judgment. Consider a Martian scientist investigating humans who observed that some individual knows both English and modern physics. From his point of view, there would be little reason to expect, on general grounds, that the learning of physics was an intellectual achievement of an incomparably higher order, that it required generations of genius; while the normal child discovers the structure of English with no difficulty. Observing this, he would conclude that one system is fitted to the human mind in a way in which the other is not. What of the system of beliefs concerning the structure of personality, the social world, human action and motives, the behavior of physical objects? It is an entirely open question whether these systems are constructed on the basis of distinct innate schemata or whether there are overriding characteristics of mind that integrate and underlie these systems.

Intrinsic principles of mental organization permit the construction of rich systems of knowledge and belief on the basis of scattered evidence. Such principles, which constitute an essential part of human nature, also determine which systems will be more accessible to the inquiring mind, and may, indeed, impose absolute limits on what can be known. An American transcendentalist speculated that "It was the design of Providence that the infant mind should possess the germ of every science. If it were not so, they could hardly be learned."[33] Charles Sanders Peirce argued that "man's mind has a natural adaptation to imagining correct theories of some kinds. . . . If man had not had the gift . . . of a mind adapted to his requirements, he . . . could not have acquired any knowledge."[34] The limits of human knowledge, he proposed, are determined by the rules that limit admissible hypotheses, which might conceivably be fairly restrictive. This is a perfectly intelligible idea.

The image of a mind, initially unconstrained, striking out freely in arbitrary directions, suggests at first

[33] Sampson Reed, *Observations on the Growth of the Mind,* 5th ed. (Boston: Crosby, Nichols, and Company, 1859), p. 45. I am indebted for this reference to Howard Zinn.

[34] "The Logic of Abduction," in Vincent Tomas, ed., *Peirce's Essays in the Philosophy of Science* (New York: Liberal Arts Press, 1957), pp. 238, 244. For further discussion, see my *Language and Mind.*

glance a richer and more hopeful view of human freedom and creativity, but I think that this conclusion is mistaken. Russell was correct in titling his study *Human Knowledge: Its Scope and Limits*. The principles of mind provide the scope as well as the limits of human creativity. Without such principles, scientific understanding and creative acts would not be possible. If all hypotheses are initially on a par, then no scientific understanding can possibly be achieved, since there will be no way to select among the vast array of theories compatible with our limited evidence and, by hypothesis, equally accessible to the mind. One who abandons all forms, all conditions and constraints, and merely acts in some random and entirely willful manner is surely not engaged in artistic creation, whatever else he may be doing. "The spirit of poetry, like all living powers, must of necessity circumscribe itself by rules," Coleridge wrote, perhaps "under laws of its own origination." If, as Russell frequently expressed it, man's "true life" consists "in art and thought and love, in the creation and contemplation of beauty and in the scientific understanding of the world,"[35] if this is "the true glory of man," then it is the intrinsic principles of mind that should be the object of our awe and, if possible, our inquiry. In investigating some of the most familiar achievements of human intelligence—the ordinary use of language, for example—we are struck at once by their creative character, by the character of free creation within a system of rule. Russell wrote that "the human-

---

[35] Bertrand Russell, in collaboration with Dora Russell, *The Prospects of Industrial Civilization* (New York and London: The Century Company, 1923), pp. 40–41.

istic conception regards a child as a gardener regards a young tree, i.e., as something with a certain intrinsic nature, which will develop into an admirable form, given proper soil and air and light."[36] I think it is fair to say that it is the humanistic conception of man that is advanced and given substance as we discover the rich systems of invariant structures and principles that underlie the most ordinary and humblest of human accomplishments.

[36] *Ibid.*, pp. 274–75.

— 2 —

On Changing the World

AT THE CONCLUSION of my first lecture, I quoted Bertrand Russell's remark that "the humanistic conception regards a child as a gardener regards a young tree, i.e., as something with a certain intrinsic nature, which will develop into an admirable form, given proper soil and air and light." Elsewhere, he developed this image further, observing that "the soil and the freedom required for a man's growth are immeasurably more difficult to discover and to obtain. . . . And the full growth which may be hoped for cannot be defined or demonstrated; it is subtle and complex, it can only be felt by a delicate intuition and dimly apprehended by imagination and respect."[1]

[1] Bertrand Russell, *Principles of Social Reconstruction* (London: George Allen & Unwin, 1916), p. 25. Where not otherwise identified, the following quotes are taken from this book and others written during World War I or shortly after, specifically, *Proposed Roads to Freedom—Anarchy, Socialism and Syndicalism* (New York: Henry Holt & Co., 1919); *Political Ideals*

Like many others who have attempted to develop a humanistic conception of man, with due respect for man's intrinsic nature and the admirable form it might achieve, Russell inclined towards libertarian concepts of education and social organization. Education, he urged, "should not aim at a passive awareness of dead facts, but at an activity directed towards the world that our efforts are to create." It should be guided by "the spirit of reverence" for "something sacred, indefinable, unlimited, something individual and strangely precious, the growing principle of life, an embodied fragment of the dumb striving of the world." Its goal should be "to elicit and fortify . . . whatever creative impulse a man may possess." Our approach to social institutions must be undertaken in the same spirit. "In the modern world, the principle of growth in most men and women is hampered by institutions inherited from a simpler age." The radical reconstruction of society must search for ways to liberate the creative impulse, not to establish new forms of authority.

Russell, I am sure, would have agreed with Wilhelm von Humboldt that "to inquire and to create—these are the centres around which all human pursuits more or less directly revolve":

> . . . all moral culture springs solely and immediately from the inner life of the soul, and can only be stimulated in human nature, and never produced by external and artificial contrivances. . . .

(New York & London: The Century Company, 1917); *The Practice and Theory of Bolshevism* (London: George Allen & Unwin, 1920) ; and *The Prospects of Industrial Civilization* (New York and London: The Century Company, 1923).

Whatever does not spring from a man's free choice, or is only the result of instruction and guidance, does not enter into his very being, but still remains alien to his true nature; he does not perform it with truly human energies, but merely with mechanical exactness.[2]

Regarding human nature in this light, one may proceed to conceive of social forms that will encourage the truly human action that grows from inner impulses. Then

all peasants and craftsmen might be elevated into artists; that is, men who love their labour for its own sake, improve it by their own plastic genius and inventive skill, and thereby cultivate their intellect, ennoble their character, and exalt and refine their pleasures. And so humanity would be ennobled by the very things which now, though beautiful in themselves, so often serve to degrade it.[3]

In the same spirit, Peter Kropotkin, expressing ideas to which Russell frequently referred, wrote that

overwork is repulsive to human nature—not work. Overwork for supplying the few with luxury—not work for the well-being of all. Work, labor, is a physiological necessity, a necessity of spending accumulated bodily energy, a necessity which is health and life itself.[4]

[2] Wilhelm von Humboldt, *The Limits of State Action,* ed. J. W. Burrow, Cambridge Studies in the History and Theory of Politics (Cambridge: Cambridge University Press, 1969), pp. 76, 63, 28.

[3] *Ibid.,* p. 27.

[4] "Anarchist Communism," quoted by Bertrand Russell in *Proposed Roads to Freedom,* p. 100.

Elaborating, Russell adds that "if men had to be tempted to work instead of driven to it, the obvious interest of the community would be to make work pleasant," and social institutions would be organized to this end. One who conceives of the "species character" of man as "free conscious activity" and "productive life," in the words of the early Marx, will also seek to create the higher form of society that Marx envisioned, in which "labor has become not only a means of life, but also the highest want in life." Russell cites approvingly a pamphlet of the National Guilds League which admits that "there is a cant of the Middle Ages, and a cant of 'joy in labor,'" but declares nevertheless that "it were better, perhaps, to risk that cant" than to accept a philosophy that makes "work a purely commercial activity, a soulless and a joyless thing."

With Humboldt and later proponents of libertarian ideas concerning man's nature and the social organization that might provide the soil and the freedom for free and healthy growth, Russell opposed the intervention in everyday life of external authority, such as the state, which tends to "make man an instrument to serve its arbitrary ends, overlooking his individual purposes."[5] But, going beyond the libertarian thought of the preindustrial period, Russell knew that the state is by no means the sole enemy of liberty.

Russell's opposition to coercive educational practice was linked to his desire for a radical reconstruction of society, "a sweeping away of all the sources of oppression, a liberation of men's constructive energies, and a wholly new way of conceiving and regulating produc-

[5] Humboldt, *Limits of State Action*, p. 69.

tion and economic relations." He retained a fundamental optimism that education could overcome the ignorance that "secures popular support for what is evil." In concluding his Nobel Prize lecture in 1950, he said:

> . . . the main thing needed to make the world happy is intelligence. And this, after all, is an optimistic conclusion, because intelligence is a thing that can be fostered by known methods of education.[6]

These words reiterated a life-long faith. Thirty years before he had written:

> Amid the myths and hysterias of opposing hatreds it is difficult to cause truth to reach the bulk of the people, or to spread the habit of forming opinions on evidence rather than on passion. Yet it is ultimately upon these things, not upon any political panacea, that the hopes of the world must rest.

Industrial civilization leads to concentration of power and the decline of individual liberty, but at the same time it frees men from the worst forms of servitude, the burden of stupefying labor, and makes it possible to imagine a world of free men who will achieve the "liberation of the creative impulse" that is the true end of social reconstruction. By increasing standards of comfort and access to information it creates conditions favorable for a radical challenge to "the old bonds of authority."

> . . . men will no longer submit merely because their forefathers did so, a reason is demanded for abstaining from claiming one's rights, and the rea-

[6] Bertrand Russell, "What Desires Are Politically Important?" in Horst Frenz, ed., *Nobel Lectures: Literature 1901–1967* (Amsterdam, London, New York: Elsevier Publishing Company, 1969), p. 463.

sons offered are counterfeit reasons, convincing
only to those who have a selfish interest in being
convinced. This condition of revolt exists in women
towards men, in oppressed nations towards their
oppressors, and above all in labour towards capital.
It is a state full of danger, as all past history shows,
yet also full of hope, if only the revolt of the
oppressed can result in victory without too terrible
a struggle, and their victory can result in the establishment of a stable social order.

The imperatives of industrial society may bring a form
of state socialism to all great states, Russell predicted in
1923. The same course of social evolution may lead the
working man to understand that he can take control of
the institutions of modern society and can become
"dependent only upon the community of fellow-workers,
not upon the arbitrary will of a special set of privileged
beings, the capitalists," or the "official caste" of a state
socialist bureaucracy. What Russell held to be necessary
was an extensive effort at persuasion and education: "it
is in the United States, as the leading capitalist nation,
that this reasonable propaganda of socialist opinion is
most needed."

Russell believed that "socialism, like everything else
that is vital, is rather a tendency than a strictly definable
body of doctrine." It should, therefore, undergo constant
change as society evolves. Furthermore, it will be
achieved, if at all, by gradual steps. Socialism presupposes the institutional structures of an advanced industrial society, in which the commitment to democracy is
already firm and widespread. Reforms should be directed
towards establishing an "industrial federal democracy,"
in which the centralized power of the state is overcome

by smaller self-governing units, in part territorial, in part industrial, along with other forms of association. Russell saw the movement for workers' control in industry as the best approach to communism. If the ground is prepared by widespread technical and business education, self-government in industry will preserve and extend democracy and avoid a technical breakdown of production. In preparation for that time, "If we have courage and patience, we can think the thoughts and feel the hopes by which, sooner or later, men will be inspired."

For the establishment of a successful communism, "men must be persuaded to the attempt by hope, not driven to it by despair." They must be persuaded to overcome the irrational impulses of nationalism and blind faith in the mythology of capitalism and other authoritarian forms. They must abandon "the belief in the importance of production" in itself, a "mania" that "has a fanatical irrationality and ruthlessness," that is destroying the earth's resources "with a reckless prodigality which entails almost a certainty of hardship for future generations," and that has turned men's thoughts away from realizing the good that could come from the opportunities for "more science and art, more diffused knowledge and mental cultivation, more leisure for wage-earners, and more capacity for intelligent pleasures." If men can be persuaded of the inherent value of self-government and creative life, they can advance towards a more humane society without the revolutionary violence which "in a democracy is infinitely dangerous," and might destroy the delicate fabric of civilized life.

Anarchism is "the ultimate ideal to which society

should approximate." For the present, Russell regarded some variant of guild socialism as a reasonable prospect for the advanced industrial societies, with workers' control of industry, a democratic parliament representing the community, some restricted forms of state management, a guarantee to all of the material necessities of a decent existence, and "the organization of citizens with special interests into groups, determined to preserve autonomy as regards their internal affairs, willing to resist interference by a strike if necessary, and sufficiently powerful (either in themselves or through their power of appealing to public sympathy) to be able to resist the organized forces of government successfully when their cause is such as many men think just."

Such ideas stand in sharp contrast to a widespread view that "All social democratic ideals fundamentally relate to how we distribute our wealth and allocate our resources: that is what socialism is about."[7] For Russell. what socialism is about is the liberation of the creative impulse and the reconstruction of society to this end. Wealth might be distributed equitably in a prison, and resources allocated rationally by a dictatorship or corporate oligarchy. Social democratic ideals are concerned with freedom, and as R. H. Tawney put the matter during World War I:

> Freedom, to be complete, must carry with it not merely the absence of repression but also the opportunity of self-organization. It must confer the right to associate with others in building up a social organization with a consciousness and corporate life of its own. Economic freedom must develop, in

[7] Anthony Crosland, "The Anti-growth Heresy," *New Statesman,* January 8, 1971, p. 39.

short, through the applications of representative institutions to industry.[8]

"There can be no real freedom or democracy," Russell wrote, "until the men who do the work in a business also control its management." Socialism will be achieved only insofar as all social institutions, in particular the central industrial, commercial, and financial institutions of a modern society, are placed under democratic control in a federal industrial republic of the sort that Russell and others envisioned, with actively functioning workers' councils and other self-governing units in which each citizen, in Thomas Jefferson's words, will be "a direct participator in the government of affairs." The organization of production and distribution, economic and social planning must be under direct democratic control in the work-place and the community if socialist ideals are to be realized. Accordingly, revolutionary movements have, quite generally, moved spontaneously to some form of council system that undertakes to place workers in direct control of production and to create "a new public space for freedom which was constituted and organized during the course of the revolution itself."[9] The destruction of these efforts by alien force

[8] R. H. Tawney, "The Conditions of Economic Liberty," *The Radical Tradition*, ed. Rita Hinden (New York: Pantheon Books, 1964), p. 103.

[9] Hannah Arendt, *On Revolution* (New York: The Viking Press, 1963), p. 253. She notes further that these spontaneous developments have been neglected even by historians sympathetic to the revolutionary movements. For similar observations, see Arthur Rosenberg, *A History of Bolshevism from Marx to the First Five Years' Plan*, trans. Ian F. Morrow (New York: Russell and Russell, Publishers, 1965). Arendt, it should be noted, believes that councils should keep to politics and not become workers' councils.

or by the power of the centralized state has, in each case, signaled the end of the socialist revolution, at least in the sense in which Russell and other libertarian thinkers conceived of socialism.

Russell's general approach to this range of topics seems to me eminently reasonable, and—after half a century of tragedy—as remote as ever from any likelihood of achievement. "The real obstacles," Russell thought, "lie in the heart of man, and the cure for these is a firm hope, informed and fortified by thought." Perhaps, in some sense, this is true. But the obstacles are immense and the means for overcoming them still slight and frail.

In the academic social sciences, in the United States at least, these questions scarcely exist. When this year's Nobel Prize winner in economics considers the range of possible economic systems, he sees a spectrum with complete *laissez faire* at one extreme and "totalitarian dictatorship of production" at the other. Assuming this framework, "the relevant choice for policy today" is to determine where along this spectrum our economy should properly lie.[10] No doubt one can place economic systems along this scale. There are other dimensions, however, along which Samuelson's polar opposites fall at the same extreme: for example, the spectrum that places direct democratic control of production at one pole and autocratic control, whether by state or private capital, at the other. In this case, as so often, the formulation of the range of alternatives narrowly constrains "the relevant choice for policy."

[10] Paul Samuelson, *Economics*, 6th ed. (New York: McGraw-Hill Book Company, 1964), p. 39.

The convergence of the great industrial systems to some form of state capitalism or state socialism—a particular form of autocratic control of production—has proceeded somewhat along the lines that Russell foresaw. Half a century later, one can see still more clearly the "extreme similarity between the Bolshevik commissary and the American Trust magnate . . . both . . . imbued with the importance of mechanism for its own sake, and of their own position as holders of the key to the clockwork." Even at the ideological level, the similarity of doctrine is impressive. The vanguard party declares itself the repository of all truth, the authentic representative of the interest of the masses. Its claims might be expressed in the words of J. P. Morgan and Company partner George W. Perkins, who explained, sixty years ago, that "the officers of the great corporation instinctively lose sight of the interest of any one individual and work for what is the broadest, most enduring interest of the many"; from the "commanding heights" of industrial life, they can take "the point of view of an intelligent, well-posted and fair arbitrator," becoming statesmen, not mere businessmen.[11] Carl Kaysen describes the modern corporation in these terms:

> No longer the agent of proprietorship seeking to maximise return on investment, management sees itself as responsible to stockholders, employees, customers, the general public, and, perhaps, most important, the firm itself as an institution . . . there is no display of greed or graspingness; there is no

[11] Cited by James Weinstein, *The Corporate Ideal in the Liberal State: 1900–1918* (Boston: Beacon Press, 1968), p. 10. Perkins was also a director of United States Steel and International Harvester.

attempt to push off on to workers or the community at large part of the social costs of the enterprise. The modern corporation is a soulful corporation.[12] Similarly, the vanguard party is a soulful party. In both cases, those who urge that men submit to the rule of these benevolent autocracies "may justly be suspected of misunderstanding human nature, and of wishing to make men into machines"—in Humboldt's words—if, indeed, the humanistic conception of human nature is correct, and the very nature of man is "to inquire and to create" under the conditions of "the freedom which awakens spontaneous activity."[13]

As late as 1922, Lenin insisted upon "this elementary truth of Marxism, that the victory of socialism requires the joint efforts of workers in a number of advanced countries."[14] He could not have been more right. There has been nothing anywhere that one might optimistically describe as a victory of socialism, at least in the libertarian sense. In parts of the underdeveloped world, where most of the population lives at what a Chinese poet once called "the zero degree of life,"[15] dramatic and exciting changes are in progress under leadership that East and West alike call "communist." The efforts to awaken the consciousness and creative forces of the peasant masses of the Third World and direct their

[12] Cited by Ralph Miliband, *The State in Capitalist Society* (New York: Basic Books, 1969), p. 31 n., among many other statements of a similar sort.

[13] Humboldt, *Limits of State Action,* pp. 24, 76, 136.

[14] Quoted in Moshe Lewin, *Lenin's Last Struggle* (New York: Pantheon Books, 1968), p. 4.

[15] Tsang K'o-chia, cited by Keith Buchanan, *Transformation of the Chinese Earth* (New York: Praeger Publishers, 1970), p. 98.

energies to modernization and development deserve
warm sympathy and respect, and, were it possible to
imagine, material support from the industrial powers.
We can only speculate as to what these efforts might
achieve, in time. It is, however, obvious that they have
not led to a society of free producers, who organize
production and distribution without external authority
and control democratically all social institutions. This
is hardly surprising, given the objective conditions that
Third World revolutions must endure, conditions in
part imposed by Western malice. The response of
Western industrial societies to revolution in the underdeveloped countries has been contemptible. Recogniz-
ing this, it remains a serious error to think of, say, Asian
communism as presenting a model for an advanced
industrial society, much as one should, in my opinion,
sympathize with many of its aspirations, much as one
must admire the heroic resistance to imperialist violence
and terror.

In the industrial societies, the prospects for libertarian socialism have hardly advanced since Russell
wrote. There is no reason to doubt the "elementary
truth" that the victory of socialism, in a truly hopeful
form, requires the joint efforts of workers in a number
of advanced countries. One may debate the extent to
which the tyranny of the Russian state derives from
Bolshevik doctrine, or from the circumstances of its
development. To describe it as "socialist" is a cruel
joke. The warnings sympathetically expressed by Russell, Rosa Luxemburg, and a few others have proved
only too accurate. A Russian anarchosyndicalist
observed in 1918 that

the proletariat is gradually being enserfed by the
state. It is being transformed into servants over
whom there has risen a new class of administrators
—a new class born mainly from the womb of the
so-called intelligentsia. . . . We do not mean to say
that . . . the Bolshevik party had set out to create a
new class system. But we do say that even the
best intentions and aspirations must inevitably be
smashed against the evils inherent in any system
of centralized power. . . . The Revolution . . . threw
itself into the arms of the old tyrant, centralized
power, which is squeezing out its life's breath. We
were too unorganized, too weak, and so we have
allowed this to happen.[16]

The author echoes a perceptive anarchist critique of
authoritarian tendencies in socialism, originating with
Bakunin. However one wishes to assign the causes, the
accuracy of the forecast is not in doubt; by now, the
"new class" is familiar to the point of cliché.

In the United States, the Pentagon system, which is
deeply embedded in American society, has been accu-
rately described as the second largest state management
in the world. Though precise details may be debated,
there is little doubt that private economic power is
heavily concentrated and that its representatives dominate the state executive, which has grown substantially
in power in the postwar years. The phenomenon has
been commonly noted and deplored. Congressional con-
servatives warn of an "elective dictatorship," echoing

[16] M. Sergven, "Paths of Revolution," *Vol'nyi Golos, Truda,*
September 1918. Reprinted in *Libertarian Analysis,* Vol. 1, No. 1
(Winter 1970). To appear in a documentary history of Russian
anarchism by Paul Avrich. Avrich suggests that "Sergven" is a
pseudonym for Gregory Maksimov.

Jefferson's early fears of "elective despotism," and speak of the drift towards "tyranny or disaster."[17] Articles with titles such as "Friendly Fascism: A Model for America" and "Fascist Democracy in the United States" have recently appeared by authors who cannot be dismissed as young radical hotheads.[18] Former Senator Joseph Clark fears that Toynbee "has much on his side" when he refers to "the progressive Germanization of the American people" as the Pentagon extends its tentacles, "reach[ing] out to take hold of a large and increasingly larger section of the gainfully employed part of the population."[19] A liberal political scientist writes:

> Put bluntly, democratic states—and the nation-state was never more than an approximation of democracy—have become less democratic in the making of policy. It has always been a wartime device in America to resolve the republic into a "constitutional dictatorship" if not a totalitarian state, vesting massive extra-constitutional powers in the executive. That necessity has become permanent, though Congress has more than once struggled with the trend and still

[17] Senator William Fulbright, quoted in the *Boston Globe*, June 20, 1969; resolution of the Senate Committee on Foreign Relations, April 16, 1969.

[18] Respectively: Bertram Gross, *Social Policy*, Vol. 1, No. 4 (November–December 1970); Daniel R. Fusfeld, Conference Reprints, Union of Radical Political Economics, No. 2. Gross is Distinguished Professor of Urban Affairs at Hunter College of the City University of New York; Fusfeld is Professor of Economics at the University of Michigan.

[19] "Asia and the Prospects for World Order," *Annals of the American Academy of Political and Social Science*, Vol. 390 (July 1970), p. 36. Clark is now National President of the World Federalists, U.S.A., and a vice-president of the Academy.

68))   *Problems of Knowledge and Freedom*

fights continual and often pointess skirmishes.[20]

A Columbia University professor of law sees the possibility of rule by "a coalition of military men, scientists, technocrats, politicians and 'realist' intellectuals who would combine a virulent anti-Communist ideology with an unrestrained primacy of military and strategic needs. It would lead to the gradual suppression of dissent and move the United States closer toward the society of 1984."[21] To correct a serious imbalance in such observations, one must emphasize that the coalition of rulers is in fact dominated by representatives of corporate interests, a point often ignored. To complete the picture, it must be stressed that these corporate interests are international in scope. K. W. Weddeburn writes: "The dominant organization of the next decade will be the multinational or international corporation," and quotes a British cabinet minister who said, in 1968, that national governments, "including the British Government, will be reduced to the status of a parish council in dealing with the large international companies which span the world."[22]

[20] Wilson C. McWilliams, "Democracy, Publics and Protest: The Problem of Foreign Policy," *Journal of International Affairs,* Vol. 23, No. 2 (1969), p. 197. See my *At War with Asia* (New York: Pantheon Books, 1970), Chap. 1, for further references and discussion.

[21] Wolfgang Friedmann, "Interventionism, Liberalism and Power Politics: The Unfinished Revolution in International Thinking," *Political Science Quarterly,* Vol. 83, No. 2 (June 1968), p. 188.

[22] "Certified Public Accountant," *New York Review of Books,* June 18, 1970, p. 23. Weddeburn is Cassel Professor of Commercial Law at the London School of Economics, and was a visiting professor at Harvard Law School when this was written.

Detailed information about this system of centralized control is limited. David Horowitz recently pointed out that he could discover no independent academic study of the impact on American social, political, or economic life of the Standard Oil Company of New Jersey—an organization that controls the economic lifeblood of half a dozen strategic countries, is a major domestic political force, has its own intelligence and paramilitary networks, and regularly provides personnel for top executive positions in the government. Robert Heilbroner has enumerated obviously central problems of American and international society that receive little academic study: analysis of the politico-economic consequences of American hegemony in foreign investment, distribution of benefits of the war economy, the means by which private wealth and income are preserved, and so on.[23] Robert Solow, commenting, attributes such gaps to "impossible difficulty" rather than "possible subversiveness." Perhaps. But there are surely grounds for skepticism.

It is interesting to contrast the scale of academic research in these areas with academic research, say, on Thailand. Writing about this matter, after some confidential and classified documents were "unearthed" by American students, Jacques Decornoy observes that the United States "has undertaken extensive studies aimed at acquiring a thorough knowledge of the workings of Thai society—with the (unstressed) aim of more easily

[23] "On the Limited Relevance of Economics," *Public Interest,* Fall 1970.

controlling them."[24] Much of this work is designed, in the wording of one academic report, "to support and strengthen the operations of the U.S. aid program in Thailand"; USAID, which administers the program, in turn has the official mission of "supporting the Royal Thai Government in its efforts to contain, control and eliminate the Communist insurgency in rural areas," this being an essential component of American policy in Southeast Asia. The object of the various research projects carried out in Thailand, Decornoy suggests, is "to lay the groundwork for bringing the Thais into the Japanese–United States sphere of influence"—an accurate judgment, the available evidence suggests.

The conclusions to be drawn from this comparison are sufficiently obvious so that little comment is necessary. The comparison illustrates the intense politicization of the American universities during the postwar years. Examples are plentiful. University laboratories— at my own university, for one—have enthusiastically devoted themselves to the design of counterinsurgency technology. The Cross-Cultural Survey of Yale University, originally set up for scientific purposes, has provided "ready-made information for intelligence and military government purposes."[25] Stanford University

[24] *Le Monde Weekly Selection,* July 22, 1970. See also Eric R. Wolf and Joseph G. Jorgensen, "Anthropology on the Warpath in Thailand," *New York Review of Books,* November 19, 1970. Some participants in the Thailand programs claim that these evaluations are unfair. The objection, of course, cannot be evaluated so long as the materials are classified or otherwise inaccessible.

[25] Wolf and Jorgensen, "Anthropology on the Warpath in Thailand," p. 32, referring to a twenty-year report of the institution.

houses and contributes to the support of the Hoover
Institution on War, Revolution and Peace, which is
required by its private benefactor to pursue the following scholarly program: "The purpose of this Institution
must be, by its research and publications, to demonstrate the evils of the doctrines of Karl Marx—whether
Communism, Socialism, economic materialism, or
atheism—thus to protect the American way of life from
such ideologies, their conspiracies, and to reaffirm the
validity of the American system." At about the same
time that this program was established, the same university—one of the best in the United States—phased
out its outstanding independent Institute of Latin
American studies; circumstantial evidence suggests that
pressure from the Ford Foundation may have been an
important factor. The director of the Institute, Professor
Ronald Hilton, seems to have offended powerful fund
raisers by the controversial opinions expressed in the
Report of the Institute—which, for example, was so
unscholarly as to reveal that the CIA was preparing an
invasion of Cuba. A Ford-funded review of the whole
affair describes the treatment of Castro's takeover in
Cuba as a major source of problems: it "made the
Stanford administration uneasy" because "it carried
the Stanford reputation behind it."[26] I do not know
whether the ideology of the Hoover Institution has
caused similar uneasiness.

The politicization of the American universities dur-

[26] This account of the Hoover Institution and the Institute of
Hispanic American and Luso-Brazilian Studies is drawn from
David Horowitz, "Sinews of Empire," *Ramparts*, October 1969,
pp. 32–42.

ing the postwar years has been sharply challenged—
properly and belatedly—by the American student movement. This is one symptom of the erosion of the cold-
war consensus that has imposed such a conservative cast
on American society since World War II. But the
attempt to convert the universities into liberal, open
institutions faces many obstacles. In the past year, there
has been a rash of firings, mostly at smaller colleges
and universities, on what appear to be strictly political
grounds. To cite one case, virtually at random, the
appointment of a philosophy instructor at Southern
Illinois University was terminated apparently because
of his opposition to a Center of Vietnamese Studies and
Programs of a highly questionable character.[27] The
chairman of the board is quoted as saying: "Mr. Allen
has criticized the university and the public knows it.
The board felt it was to the best interests of the university not to have people of that caliber on the faculty.
If Mr. Allen is unhappy at the university, we see no
reason why he should want to stay and teach there."[28]
There have been many cases of this sort in the past few
years. The purge of radical junior faculty—I believe
the term is fair—at "nonelite" institutions is one element in the general campaign to reinstitute the ideological unity and conformism of the postwar years.

It is, incidentally, interesting and somewhat ironic
that just at the moment when the subservience of the
academic world to external institutions is being ques-
tioned, the cry is raised that the universities are being

---

[27] For discussion of this Center, see *Bulletin of Concerned
Asian Scholars,* Special Issue, February 1971.

[28] *Southern Illinoisan,* October 18, 1970.

"politicized." I happen to agree with the critics who warn of the dangers of politicizing the universities, which should be, so far as possible, independent of the influence of external powers, state or private, or of militant factions within. But one notes, with interest, how rarely this fear was expressed during the period when the academic world was devoting itself to supporting and strengthening the operations of the United States aid program in Thailand or producing counterinsurgency technology and advanced guidance systems for new generations of missiles, while circumventing such problems as the impact of the Standard Oil Company on American policy.

It was not many years ago that the president of the American Historical Association, in his presidential address, argued that "dispassionate behaviorism" and "the liberal neutral attitude" in research violated the "social responsibilities of the historian." "Total war whether it be hot or cold enlists everyone and calls upon everyone to assume his part. The historian is no freer from his obligation than the physicist."[29] Though not always so openly expressed, such sentiments were widely held and rarely challenged until a few years ago. Both the physicist and the historian have, to a large extent, accepted the obligation to serve the policies and power of the state.

Peter Berger observed that "As the physicists are

[29] Conyers Read (in 1949), cited by Michael Parenti, *The Anti-Communist Impulse* (New York: Random House, 1969), p. 75. Read was wrong, incidentally, with regard to "dispassionate behaviorism," which has been perverted into an ideological instrument. See below, for some comments.

busy engineering the world's annihilation, the social scientists can be entrusted with the smaller mission of engineering the world's consent."[30] There is more than a little truth to this remark. It is significant that students have begun to ask whether they should willingly undertake to engineer the world's consent to the international order designed by the ruling circles of the great powers. Is it, for example, at all proper to carry out research on Thailand if it will be used, as undeniably it will, to prop up a particular ruling elite which, quite apart from its corruption and violence, happens also to secure the territorial base for the long-term American effort to dominate Southeast Asia? Is it not, in fact, a legitimate question whether the weight of research about a certain society should be outside of its control, available not to its members and their democratic structures (if they exist) but rather available to those who in the larger society, domestic or international, have the power to make use of this research for their own purposes? These are not trivial questions, and it is unfortunate that consideration of them has been so long delayed, and is even now so marginal to the concerns of many academic intellectuals. It is the great merit of the student movement to have insistently brought such questions to general awareness.

The willing subservience of the academic community to state power, and its decline as the Vietnam war progressed, are of some importance. It is a significant question, in an advanced industrial society, whether

[30] *Invitation to Sociology: A Humanistic Perspective* (Garden City, N.Y.: Doubleday & Company, Anchor Books, 1963), p.152.

what John Kenneth Galbraith calls "the scientific and educational estate" becomes an independent (hence often dissenting or even revolutionary) force, or, alternatively, accepts its role in social management. If the "technical intelligentsia" comes to see itself as part of the work force of an advanced society and devotes itself to "structural reforms"—in Andre Gorz's phrase—that "create new centers of democratic power," the social impact might be significant. Radical transformation of any society is unthinkable without the active participation of those engaged in creative and productive work. In an advanced industrial society, the "scientific and educational establishment" can be a crucial element in social progress. One factor in the betrayal of the promise of socialist revolution has been the willingness of the technical intelligentsia to assimilate itself to a new ruling class, a process that bears comparison to the eager acceptance, in Western democracies, of a role in the expanding state management. But industrial civilization creates a technical intelligentsia that is not only extensive in scale but also increasingly a central element in the work force. Conceivably, this "proletarianization of the intellectuals" may eliminate the role of the professional revolutionary intellectual with his vanguard party that expresses the interests of the inarticulate masses lacking in consciousness. It might, conceivably, make possible a new revolutionary movement in which, as skilled labor, state employment, service and administrative occupations, technology, and science absorb the mass of the work force, intellectual and manual workers will not be so sharply separated as in the past, and the declining necessity for men to serve as tools of production will blur distinctions that have aborted earlier attempts to place the central institutions of an industrial society under democratic control.[31] At the very least this tendency might aid in the formation of a movement of social reform along lines discussed by John Kenneth Galbraith and Michael Harrington, for example. In the United States, this would be a development of some significance, much as it would fall short of what might, in principle, be achieved for human liberation under the material conditions of advanced industrial society.

There is a fair amount of skepticism about the possibilities of significant reform in the United States, and not only among radicals. Hans Morgenthau, for one, has recently given an analysis of the crisis of American society that might almost be read as a call for revolution, though it was no doubt intended as an expression of despair:

> . . . it should by now have become obvious that the great issues of our day—the militarization of American life, the Vietnam war, race conflicts, poverty, the decay of the cities, the destruction of the natural environment—are not susceptible to rational solutions within the existing system of power relations. . . . Poverty on a large scale, like the decay of the cities and the ruination of the natural environment, is a result not of accidental misfortunes but of social and economic policies in whose continuation powerful social groups have a

[31] Discussions of these possibilities are too numerous to enumerate. See, for example, Andre Gorz, *Strategy for Labor* (Boston: Beacon Press, 1967); Alain Touraine, *The Post-industrial Society* (New York: Random House, 1971); Norman Birnbaum, *The Crisis of Industrial Society* (New York: Oxford University Press, 1969); and many other studies.

vested interest. . . . In brief, the overriding single issue, of which all the others are but specific manifestations, is the distribution of power in American society. . . .

This distribution of power has survived, essentially undisturbed, all movements for reform—movements which "appear in retrospect as essentially futile attempts at accomplishing through rational and moderate reform what can be accomplished only by a radical shift of power and priorities, either through the disintegration of the existing power structure or through revolution." American society has chosen to reject its rhetorical commitment to equality in freedom and to use all the means at its disposal to preserve the existing system of injustice, at home and abroad, as its "ultimate purpose," so Morganthau concludes. Our fear of Communism and "our conformist subservience to those in power" are responsible for the betrayal of the promise of American society.[32]

One might go further. A case can be made that these movements for reform did not aim for redistribution of power in the first place, but rather have historically represented "the political ideology of the rising, and then dominant, business groups," and that "few reforms were enacted without the tacit approval, if not the guidance, of the large corporate interests."[33]

Nevertheless, even such dire assessments as Morgenthau's should not be read as implying that a mass reform movement would have no place in American

[32] "The End of the Republic?" *New York Review of Books*, September 24, 1970, pp. 39–40.

[33] Weinstein, *The Corporate Ideal*, p. ix.

politics. On the contrary, it might impede the growth of militarized state capitalism and some of the worst atrocities, such as the Indochina war, and perhaps begin to undertake the "reasonable propaganda of socialist opinion" which, as Russell noted, is so urgently needed in the United States.

There is a possibility that a mass reform movement would absorb some of the energies that might be devoted to more radical social change: the danger of "cooptation," which not even the most radical program can escape. The problem has received lively discussion in connection with the recent revival of interest in workers' control of industry;[34] so it must, as we see when we read, in the only book on the subject published in the United States, about the importance of council organization for those "concerned with ways of eliciting improved effort and performance," "exploring new ways of training and supervising a workforce," and seeking "new procedures to develop discipline and to settle complaints or dissipate protest": for such reasons, "The range of experience with workers' councils provides a record of general interest to those shaping or modifying industrial relations and economic institutions."[35] In fact, it has even been argued that Marxism served primarily to "socialize" the proletariat and integrate it more effectively into industrial society, so that the revolutionary movement contributed to the creation

[34] See, for example, *The Debate on Workers' Control,* Institute for Workers' Control, 1970; "The Ambiguities of 'Workers' Control,' " *Solidarity,* Vol. 6, No. 6 (October 15, 1970).

[35] John T. Dunlop, introduction to Adolf Sturmthal, *Workers' Councils* (Cambridge, Mass.: Harvard University Press, 1964), p. v.

of a "race of patient and disciplined workers."[36] Those who oppose a program of social action merely on grounds that it might be "coopted" doom themselves to paralysis: they are opposed to everything imaginable.

Largely under the impact of the student and black liberation movements, the United States has been awakening slowly from the dogmatic slumber of the postwar years. It would be difficult to find any serious sociologist today who would announce that "the fundamental political problems of the industrial revolution have been solved";[37] and the general perception of the American role in international affairs has also been drastically modified. In fact, liberal opinion has adopted many positions of the "New Left revisionism" of just a few years ago.[38] It remains to be seen to what extent these new-found opportunities for rational discussion of the problems of industrial society and the American world role will be preserved, and exploited.

There is little reason for optimism in this regard, despite the real changes of the past few years. The cold-war ideology, after all, had a real function in postwar American society. It was not merely a mass para-

[36] Arthur Redford, quoted by Adam B. Ulam on pp. 66–67 of *The Unfinished Revolution: An Essay on the Sources of Influence of Marxism and Communism* (New York: Random House, 1960), where this thesis is developed.

[37] Seymour Martin Lipset, *Political Man: The Social Bases of Politics* (Garden City, N.Y.: Doubleday & Company, 1960), p. 406.

[38] See, for example, Adam Yarmolinsky, "The Military Establishment," *Foreign Policy,* Winter 1970–1971, pp. 78–79. He of course continues to berate "the historical revisionists of the New Left" (without reference), following the literary convention for articles of this sort.

noia, inexplicable and aberrant. William A. Williams outlined this function succinctly when he wrote that after World War II, American power

> was adroitly deployed behind the banner of anti-communism, a psychological and political strategy that was as successful as it was commonplace. The imperial majority of American leaders recognized that the populace would have to be re-aroused to sustain the kind of activity (and its related costs) that they had supported during the war. Senator Arthur Vandenberg was merely being more candid than most of his colleagues when he remarked that it would be necessary 'to scare hell out of the American people.' The specter of communism met that need.[39]

It met that need not only for the American people but for their leaders as well. As former Undersecretary of the Air Force Townsend Hoopes relates, the policy makers of the Kennedy administration operated on "the implicit assumption that henceforth Washington would be predisposed to view an effort to overthrow the existing order *anywhere* as a national-liberation war fomented by and for the benefit of Russia or China," and Johnson's advisers (Kennedy appointees) "all carried in their veins the implicitly unlimited commitment to global struggle against Revolutionary Communism." The prevailing assumption was "that the 'Communist

[39] "The Large Corporation and American Foreign Policy," in David Horowitz, ed., *Corporations and the Cold War* (New York: Monthly Review Press and the Bertrand Russell Foundation, 1969), p. 100. Another figure who was more candid than most was Dean Acheson. For some discussion, see Ronald Steel, "Commissar of the Cold War," *New York Review of Books,* February 12, 1970, pp. 15–21.

Bloc' remained an essentially cohesive international conspiracy manifesting itself primarily in military and
paramilitary assaults against that other comprehensible
entity, the 'Free World.' "[40] So we find Walt Rostow
and Dean Acheson pretending that the Vietnamese
revolution, the war against French colonialism, was
fomented by Stalin, and to this day it remains an article
of faith that Stalin was responsible for the Greek civil
war and that the Communist parties of the world,
immediately after World War II, "were bent on widespread disruption." Moreover, Hoopes explains, those
"who still value reason and believe in factual, propor-
tioned discourse as the most reliable road to approximate truth" will reject, with no further discussion, the
idea that the American leadership was "acting within
the compulsions of an imperialist system."[41] It is particularly interesting that these sentiments are expressed
in an essay that is intended to extricate us from the
fantasies of the postwar years. In fact, it is widely
accepted doctrine that the United States is thus fundamentally different from all other great powers in history.
Many American intellectuals would see nothing odd in
Sidney Hook's contention that "Where United States
actions are to be faulted, they resulted from mistaken
assessments of the foreign military and paramilitary
forces at work."[42] It is only other powers that act in the
"national interest" or the perceived self-interest of rul-

[40] Townsend Hoopes, *The Limits of Intervention* (New
York: David McKay Co., 1969), pp. 15, 16, 8.

[41] Townsend Hoopes, "Legacy of the Cold War in Indochina," *Foreign Affairs,* Vol. 48, No. 4 (July 1970), pp. 602, 601.

[42] Sidney Hook, "The Knight of the Double Standard,"
The Humanist, Vol. 21, No. 1 (January–February 1971), p. 32.

ing groups. But when the United States attacks Indochina with (by now) almost three times the tonnage of bombs used by the American Air Force in all theaters in World War II, or when it invades the Dominican Republic, or supports the overthrow of the government of Guatemala, these actions, insofar as they are objectionable, must be attributed to mistaken analysis of the facts.

Or consider Eugene Rostow, another Kennedy adviser. He explains, with apparent seriousness, that if the United States does not maintain its position of dominance in Southeast Asia by winning the war in Vietnam, an inexorable process will be set off that may ultimately reduce it to the status of Finland, subject to Russian will. The United States would not become Poland, he admits, "but we would begin to move toward that kind of posture." He goes on to explain that if we do not control South Vietnam, there is a danger that we might set off a nuclear war out of fear of Russian hegemony, surely the most astonishing argument that has ever been advanced by an apologist for imperialism.[43] Or we have William Bundy, another Kennedy adviser, who sees the American war in Indochina as a valiant effort to prevent the East Wind of China from blowing down the dominoes. That the Chinese were mysteriously absent from this drama seems to disturb him not at all. The big problem is this: "Will China *once again* threaten pressure and subversion?" (my italics). And Bundy suspects not, because "Mao and his colleagues have been impressed during the last five years by America's evident

[43] Eugene Rostow, quoted by William Whitworth in "A Reporter at Large: Interview with Eugene V. Rostow," *New Yorker,* July 4, 1970, pp. 30–56.

desire to avoid war with China; the whole experience [of Vietnam] is one of the elements that may make an easing of tension and growth of communication now possible."[44] This eminent commentator, formerly Assistant Secretary of State for Far Eastern Affairs, leaves it to the reader to draw the obvious conclusion for improving Russian-American relations. Following his logic, we should bomb Hungary into rubble, so that the Russians will better appreciate our evident desire to avoid a nuclear war, and will then join in easing tension and extending communication.

Despite such examples, which can be enumerated at length, it is fair to say that the system of beliefs that muted political debate for twenty years is no longer tenable. Few literate people are willing to believe that domestic communists are a threat to American freedom or that there is a monolithic conspiracy directed from Moscow or Peking that will reduce the United States to the status of Finland or Poland if it abandons its global military efforts. Unfortunately, these steps towards sanity are still not generally accompanied by a willingness to apply to American policy the intellectual standards taken for granted elsewhere.

The erosion of the cold-war ideology is a serious matter. It served well as a technique for mobilizing the American population in support of national policy. The domestic programs of government-induced, largely military production and related research (which involved close to two-thirds of the country's scientists and engineers and a large part of the labor force) have undoubt-

[44] William Bundy, "New Tides in Southeast Asia," *Foreign Affairs,* Vol. 49, No. 2 (January 1971), p. 191.

edly been a major factor in preserving "economic health." They were tolerated by the taxpayer in part because his leaders succeeded in scaring hell out of him —at a fearsome social cost. The specter of communism also met the need to mobilize the American people in support of long-standing international objectives, specifically, to "open the doors of all the weaker countries to an invasion of American capital and enterprise," in the words of Woodrow Wilson's Secretary of State, in 1914, stating the official policy of the administration.[45]

These objectives have not changed. There appears to be no serious move towards dismantling the system of militarized state capitalism or towards abandoning the effort to "contain," where possible, independent development on the part of societies attempting to extricate themselves from the international system largely dominated by the United States. Since the ideology of anti-communism no longer serves to mobilize the population, there will be, it is safe to predict, a search for some new technique of social control, perhaps a continuing effort to replace the no longer credible communist threat by some terrifying image of left-wing students allied with ethnic minorities and Third World revolutionaries, threatening to tear down the pillars of civilized society. It is hardly surprising that some of the people who helped convert a justified opposition to "communist" totalitarianism into a paranoid anti-communist crusade are now attacking the student movement with the techniques of distortion, innuendo, and exaggeration, and with some success.

[45] William Jennings Bryan, cited by Williams, "The Large Corporation and American Foreign Policy," p. 85.

In fact, student activism has predominantly been related to the issues of racism and war. As to the latter, the presidential reports and commissions have been unanimous, and of course correct, in relating student activism to the Vietnam war. The reaction to these conclusions on the part of the state executive and its spokesmen is quite interesting: it has been an endeavor to dissociate campus protest from the war. The logic is clear. The administration is hoping to be able to conduct a long-haul, low-cost effort in Indochina, which could go on indefinitely. Therefore, it is necessary to reduce the cost. But a major cost is the bitterness and alienation of the youth. This is tied to the Vietnam war and cannot be alleviated as long as the war continues. Therefore, one must deny that this is a cost of the war. Rather, student unrest is caused by drugs, or radical professors, or Doctor Spock, or spineless administrators, or social permissiveness. The attempt to dissociate student protest from its social context parallels the effort to conjure up some new demon to frighten the population back into the convenient passivity of the 1950s.

For the people of Indochina, all of this is no game, but a matter of survival. Outside of the student movement, there is no substantial group that has taken a principled stand on the war. By this I refer to opposition to the war not on grounds of its cost, or failure, or remoteness from the national interest, or even its savagery, but rather opposition that is based on the same considerations that led to universal revulsion over the Russian invasion of Czechoslovakia: quick, relatively bloodless, supported by part of the population, and successful in imposing the rule of Czech collaborators so that most Russian troops could be withdrawn—a paradigm example of successful "Vietnamization." I mean opposition based on the principle that no great power—not even one so selfless and beneficent as the United States—has the authority or the competence to determine by force the social and political structure of Vietnam or any other country, no right to serve as international judge and executioner.

The record of the intellectual community, as I have already mentioned, has not been a proud one. Telford Taylor, former chief United States counsel at Nuremberg and now Professor of Law at Columbia University, is quite correct in saying that "The war, in the massive, lethal dimensions it acquired after 1964 [and, though he does not recognize the fact, well before], was the work of highly educated academics and administrators, most of whom would fit rather easily the present Vice President's notion of an 'effete snob.' It was . . . the Rusks, McNamaras, Bundys, and Rostows . . . who must bear major responsibility for the war and the course it took." It is such men who are responsible for the "mad cerebrations" that have led to the destruction of Indochina, and who, he implies, should be judged by the principles of Nuremberg if we are to be honest with ourselves.[46] One must agree with the judgment of

[46] Telford Taylor, *Nuremberg and Vietnam: An American Tragedy* (Chicago: Quadrangle Books, 1970), p. 205. For a still more explicit statement by Taylor, see *New York Times,* January 9, 1971. At the same time, Taylor reveals the essential moral weakness of the Nuremberg proceedings. The American bombardment of North Vietnam, he argues, cannot be regarded as a violation of the laws of war, because "Aerial bombardment had been used so extensively and ruthlessly on the Allied as well as the Axis side that neither at Nuremberg nor Tokyo was the issue made a part of the trials."

Townsend Hoopes that the architects of the Vietnam tragedy were "almost uniformly, those considered when they took office to be among the ablest, the best, the most humane and liberal men that could be found for public trust."[47] And, as Taylor notes, it is leading liberal academic scholars who describe the exodus to the cities "stimulated by 'zippo' raids and air strikes, and the consequent wretched huddle in refugee camps and hospitals, as 'forced-draft urbanization and modernization' . . . a euphemism to end all euphemisms, fit to be bracketed with an American general's reported and less elegant judgment: 'If you get them by the balls, the hearts and minds will follow.' "[48]

It was under the Kennedy administration that major programs in counterinsurgency were developed, that American troops (called "advisers") were directly involved on a large scale in bombing and strafing, and that defoliation and large-scale population removal and "population control" were undertaken. The intensification of these programs under Johnson, the massive bombardment of South Vietnam, along with the direct ground invasion and the vast extension of the air war to Laos and North Vietnam, all were initiated and directed by Kennedy advisers, some of whom, in later years, turned against the war—as most of them emphasized, because of its cost and failure. But it would be a gross and self-serving error to speak only of the atrocious behavior of "the most humane and liberal men that could be found

[47] "The Nuremberg Suggestion," *Washington Monthly,* January 1970, pp. 18–21. For discussion see my *At War with Asia,* Chap. 6.
[48] Taylor, *Nuremberg and Vietnam,* pp. 202.

for public trust" or the liberal American intellectuals who helped and advised them. How many are able to escape the judgment expressed by Jan Myrdal?

> . . . the unconscious one does not betray. He walks secure through life. But we who are a part of the tradition—the Europeans—and who carry on the tradition we have betrayed with awareness, insight and consciousness, we have carefully analyzed all the wars before they were declared. But we did not stop them. (And many amongst us became the propagandists of the wars as soon as they were declared.) We describe how the poor are plundered by the rich. We live among the rich. Live on the plunder and pander ideas to the rich. We have described the torture and we have put our names under appeals against torture, but we did not stop it. (And we ourselves became torturers when the higher interests demanded torture and we became the ideologists of torture.) Now we once more can analyze the world situation and describe the wars and explain why the many are poor and hungry. But we do no more.
>
> We are not the bearers of consciousness. We are the whores of reason.[49]

There are, to be sure, exceptions. For example, the Berrigan brothers, now in prison and facing further indictments, have attempted to do more than merely expose and explain the facts of the Indochina war. But for the most part, those who do not accept the official ideology or contribute to the exercise of state power are willing to accumulate footnotes for history while permitting the democratic state to murder and destroy as it

---

[49] *Confessions of a Disloyal European* (New York: Pantheon Books, 1968), pp. 200–201.

wills. *"Argue* as much as you like and about whatever you like, but *obey!"* Such was the policy of Frederick the Great, as Kant described it. The peasants of Indochina might well ask us how much they have gained by the triumph of democracy in the West.

The latest brainchild of the counterinsurgency theorists is to solve the problems of the northern zones of South Vietnam, where the population refuses to accept government authority even in provinces that have been virtually destroyed by American force,[59] by "the largest planned movement of peasants in the history of Vietnam." "South Vietnamese officials . . . confirm that the movement could involve between two million and three million peasants." But since "they are like sheep," a Saigon minister assures us, there is no need to be concerned over their willingness to move.[51] Furthermore,

[50] For details, as of three years ago, see Jonathan Schell, *The Military Half* (New York: Random House, Vintage Books, 1968). At that time—that is, before the great expansion of the technological war in 1968—several provinces in the north were 70 percent destroyed, by reporters' estimates.

[51] *New York Times,* January 11, 1971. Added in press: In an article headed "Saigon is said to abandon big refugee re-settlement," The *New York Times,* March 12, reports that "American officials were embarrassed by the January disclosure" and that "From that point on the whole idea has been played down" (quoting an American source in Saigon). Currently cited figures on relocation, from 10,000 to 20,000 refugees, "are well below the original estimates of those involved." American officials claim that the change in plans was occasioned by a survey conducted among the refugees. Though it is virtually impossible to ascertain the facts, it may be that the public protest after these scandalous plans were revealed did cause the project to be abandoned or reduced in scale. If so, the lesson is clear. The same report notes that about one million Vietna-

he might have added, most are already refugees, so there is no real change in status involved. And who would object to leaving behind him conditions such as these?

The refugees have come in a number of ways. For one, there have been major sweeps where the US and ARVN have just gone in and rounded up everyone in the village and brought them in as refugees. People that ran away were shot as VC and people who wouldn't come of course were also VC, and shot. In the areas where they couldn't even muster enough force to get in there with helicopters to take the people out, they would just totally destroy the area. They would defoliate the rice crops. They've been bombing these areas heavily for at least five years, and hitting the land with H + I fire, which is

---

mese are living in "what are officially considered to be unviable conditions" in the northern region.

Although published reports are scanty, it is clear that forced population removal is continuing in Indochina. Tad Szulc reports that the number of war refugees in South Vietnam has increased dramatically, perhaps to five times the previous monthly rate, between October 1970 and February 1971, as a result of new US-ARVN military actions. Among them are 40,000 Montagnards and 38,000 new refugees from the U Minh Forest area, "forced out . . . as a result of B-52 raids and South Vietnamese operations" (*New York Times,* March 13). The Kennedy Subcommittee on Refugees estimates that three million refugees have been "generated" during the past two years, and this estimate is confirmed by other government sources (Herbert Mitgang, *New York Times,* March 15). While the nation agonizes over the trial of Lieutenant Calley, a new sweep in the My Lai area "may force as many as 16,000 people from their homes" (Henry Kamm, *New York Times,* April 1). Laotian hill tribesmen have been forcibly removed to South Vietnam by retreating ARVN troops, in unknown numbers (*New York Times,* March 29). As to the scale of these operations, one can only guess.

"harassment and interdiction"—that's just firing
at random all over the countryside—no aim at all.
When the situation gets bad enough that you can't
eat, then you'll move, or starve.

I know from friends that people who live in
the western part of these provinces have to live
underground—literally. All the time. They live in
caves and bunkers, and come up during the night
to grow vegetables in the bomb craters. They've
learned that certain sorts of plants grow very well
in phosphorus bomb craters; and the TNT-type
bomb has a lot of nitrogen in it, which is very good
for growing other types of plants. This is how they
survive. [They grow vegetables in the bomb cra-
ters] because there's not much left but bomb
craters.

After the population is removed, the area will no doubt
be sanitized by bombs and artillery. Hostetter predicts
that "all of the countryside in this area will be totally
obliterated. Anyone who remains will be destroyed."[52]

What will the reaction be in the democratic states of
the West to the official announcement of this new
atrocity, or to the further steps in executing it? As it
waits to see, the American executive will continue to

[52] Doug Hostetter, interview in CRV Newsletter, January
1971, 840 West Oakdale Avenue, Chicago. Hostetter, a religious
pacifist, worked as a volunteer from 1966 to 1969 in Quang Tin
province and recently returned for a short visit. He speaks Vietnamese and knows the area well. He estimates that the countryside is about 95 percent pro-NLF and the province capital (by
Vietnamese reports) 80 percent pro-NLF. The people are so
antigovernment, he reports, that when Vice-President Ky came
to visit the village in which he lived, the entire population
(except for officials) were confined to their homes: "you could
be shot just for stepping out on the streets. That's how well the
Saigon Government is loved in I corps."

prosecute alleged conspiracies against its crimes, conveniently forgetting the judgment of Nuremberg.

Bertrand Russell was one of the select few among the true bearers of consciousness. His efforts to alert the American people to the barbarism of the American war provoked widespread denunciations. A *New York Times* editorial regretted his "unthinking receptivity to the most transparent Communist propaganda"—that is, to direct reports that were, so far as we know, quite true. The *Times* went on to describe the "American advisers and trainers, whose bearing, moderation and judgment have done a great deal of good." At about that time, in 1963, the American war correspondent Richard Tregaskis, no dove, interviewed an American helicopter pilot who said:

> Down there, you have pretty solid VC areas, where you can assume everybody is an enemy. You know, the 362 [the 362d Squadron, which preceded the pilot's unit in Vietnam] were wild men. One chopper would go first, and when the people would go running, the second plane would spray 'em.[53]

Among the other forms of "doing a great deal of good" were the use of defoliation since 1961 or 1962 to drive peasants into government-controlled camps, leading often to starvation and death,[54] but with little publicity. The

[53] *Vietnam Diary* (New York: Holt, Rinehart & Winston, 1963), p. 108. On Russell's early efforts, and the editorial response, see his *War Crimes in Vietnam* (New York: Monthly Review Press, 1967).

[54] See my *At War with Asia*, Chap. 2, for some references. On American involvement in Laos at that period, see N. Adams and A. McCoy, eds., *Laos: War and Revolution* (New York: Harper & Row, 1970). Interesting reading, in this connection, is

evidence produced by the Russell Tribunal was also effectively withheld from American and British audiences; the extensive testimony was, so far as is now known, quite accurate.[55] All in all, not the most glorious chapter in the annals of the "special relationship."

In my opinion, there could be no more fitting memorial to Russell than a revival of the Tribunal that he initiated. What the Tribunal exposed is now no secret. But the war crimes continue, while the criminals concoct fantastic "conspiracies" led by imprisoned pacifist priests. As the Tribunal came to an end, its presiding officer warned that in addition to devoting every effort to save that "small nation of peasants . . . [who] have been subjected to the fury of the military machine belonging to the mightiest power in the world," it would be necessary for men of conscience to come to the defense of American war resisters, "the defenders of all that is best in the tradition of [their] country."[56] The endless American war in Asia demands passivity at home, tolerance or apathy among America's allies. If there is no one with the stature of a Bertrand Russell to

Coral Bell's "How Guilty Are American Liberals?" *New Society*, April 9, 1970, an article which entirely overlooks the nature of the American military involvement in Vietnam and Laos under Kennedy as well as the fact that it was the same liberal advisers and a president with liberal credentials to match his predecessor's who initiated the later escalation of the war.

[55] Among other books which could find no major publisher, and received virtually no reviews, is the documentary collection *In the Name of America*, edited by Seymour Melman and others (Annandale, Va.: Turnpike Press, 1968).

[56] Vladimir Dedijer, *The Battle Stalin Lost* (New York: The Viking Press, 1971), p. 331.

carry on his work, it does not follow that the task must be abandoned.

Those with a taste for the grotesque can indulge it by reviewing the various mechanisms that have been used to avoid consciousness, as the Indochina war unfolded. Perhaps it is unfair to review the efforts by state propagandists to explain the benefits we provide the Vietnamese by destroying their land and urbanizing their society. An investigating team of the American Association for the Advancement of Science recently concluded that defoliation has caused "extremely serious harm" in Vietnam: for example, perhaps half the trees in the mature hardwood forests north and west of Saigon are dead, and a massive invasion of apparently worthless bamboo threatens to take over the area for decades to come.[57] But, the Pentagon replies, "some parts of South Vietnam's economy, notably the forest industry and small farmers, might have benefited from defoliation."[58] "Parts of the hardwood forest have been destroyed and can now be lumbered. Defoliation permits easier access, so crews can go in and bring out the wood." These benefits, this spokesman might have added, will accrue for many years, since the AAAS team estimates that 6.2 billion board feet of merchantable timber have been killed by herbicides, the equivalent of South Vietnam's entire domestic timber needs for thirty-one years, at current levels. By the same logic, we must praise Hitler for his contributions to city planning in Rotterdam.

[57] The last sentence is quoted from the report in *Science,* January 8, 1971.

[58] *New York Times,* January 9, 1971. The next two sentences are quoted from Pentagon spokesman Jerry Friedheim.

Others prefer to record the faults of those designated as our enemies. For example, the Vietminh resorted to selective terror as it began to reorganize in the late 1950s, though obviously not on anything like the scale of the regime imposed by the United States. Thus Joseph Buttinger writes:

> In June 1956 Diem organized two massive expeditions to the regions that were controlled by the Communists without the slightest use of force. His soldiers arrested tens of thousands of people. . . . Hundreds, perhaps thousands of peasants were killed. Whole villages whose populations were not friendly to the government were destroyed by artillery.[59]

The terrorism of the Vietminh, as it sought to reconstitute itself after the assault of the American client government, has received much censure. I have no access to the sources, but would not be surprised to discover that many educated Japanese reacted in the same way to the terrorism of the Nationalist Chinese in the late 1930s, as "in the occupied coastal areas, Nationalist Chinese execution squads had begun to eliminate known or suspected collaborators in a grim variety of ways designed to terrorize those who cooperated with the enemy."[60] But the terrorism of the Chinese (or, say, the

[59] Translated from "Lösung für Vietnam," *Neues Forum* (Vienna), August–September 1966, by Edward S. Herman, in his *Atrocities in Vietnam* (Philadelphia: Pilgrim Press, 1970), p. 22. Buttinger was one of the earliest supporters of Diem, although he later withdrew his support. Buttinger describes the National Liberation Front as "the Vietminh reborn."

[60] John H. Boyle, "The Road to Sino-Japanese Collaboration," *Monumenta Nipponica*, Vol. 25 (1970), pp. 3–4.

French) resistance did not evoke, in the West, a cry for massive bombardment of the resistance forces.

Other inadequacies of "our enemies" receive ample attention as well. For example, one American scholar refers to the alleged "failures" of the Pathet Lao: "The claims of substantial advances do not appear to be borne out by the testimony of refugees or sympathetic observers," he writes.[61] As his sole evidence, this RAND Corporation scholar cites the reports of Jacques Decornoy, who visited the liberated zones of Laos in 1968 and described the life of the peasants hiding in caves under the ceaseless bombardment of the American air force that had destroyed their towns and villages and farms. (Decornoy's reports also did not fall into the category of "all the news that is fit to print," in the American press at least; whether the British press thought differently, I do not know.) This scholar does not present the "testimony of the refugees," who report that they were often unable to farm even at night because of the terror attacks of the organization that sponsored the study in which he reports the failure of Pathet Lao efforts at social and economic development. One recalls Russell's comments on Western attitudes towards Bolshevik failures during the "bitter and doubtful civil and external war, involving the constant menace of domestic enemies":

> Every failure of industry, every tyrannous regulation brought about by the desperate situation, is used by the Entente as a justification of its policy. If a man is deprived of food and drink, he will

[61] Paul F. Langer, *Laos: Preparing for a Settlement in Vietnam*, P-4024, RAND Corporation, February 1969.

grow weak, lose his reason, and finally die. This is not usually considered a good reason for inflicting death by starvation. But where nations are concerned, the weakness and struggles are regarded as morally culpable, and are held to justify further punishment. . . . Is it surprising that professions of humanitarian feeling on the part of English people are somewhat coldly received in Soviet Russia?[62]

I do not, however, want to press this analogy, which is far from exact. The Entente was physically, and perhaps even morally, incapable of the savagery of the American attack on Indochina.

Another effective technique of mystification has been to formulate the "problems" of the war in purely technical terms. Two experts in counterinsurgency, one American and one British, explain that "all the dilemmas [of counterinsurgency] are practical and as neutral in an ethical sense as the laws of physics."[63] The situation is a simple one. We have the goal of establishing the rule of selected social groups in the society selected for the experiment in counterinsurgency. A number of methods are available, ranging from rural development and commodity import programs to B-52s and crop destruction, and the policy maker faces the task of combining these methods in such a manner as to maximize the probability of success. Obviously only a hysteric or a self-flagellating moralist could see an ethical problem here. Academic terminology can be put to good use. Driving people into government-controlled cities by fire power and chemical

[62] Russell, *Practice and Theory of Bolshevism,* pp. 68, 55.
[63] George K. Tanham and Dennis J. Duncanson, "Some Dilemmas of Counterinsurgency," *Foreign Affairs,* Vol. 48, No. 1 (October 1969), pp. 113–22.

destruction is "urbanization," an index of modernization of the society. We carry out "experiments with
population-control measures." We disregard such mysti-
cal notions as "attitudes," and "control behavior" by
appropriate arrangement of positive and negative rein-
forcement, such as "confiscation of chickens, razing of
houses, or destruction of villages."[64] Or, consider "the
offer of food in exchange for certain services." "If this
has in the past been a strong stimulus, it can probably
be weakened by increasing local agricultural production.
If it has been a weak or neutral stimulus, it can probably be strengthened by burning crops."[65]

   Since the problems are only technical, it is an easy
step to explain atrocities in terms of stupidity and error
rather than criminal intent. To appreciate the extent and
effectiveness of this device, one can undertake the following useful exercise. Imagine that the Soviet Union had
dropped some six million tons of bombs on a faraway
land where the population was not properly following
orders. Then select some dovish Western commentary
on the Indochina war and make the appropriate substi-
tutions: "USSR" for "US," and so on. Imagine reading
an account of how the war had unfortunately "become
the solving of a series of technical problems" that had
led the "genial, efficient and unpretentious senior officers" to plan operations in which peasants had been

[64] For references, see my *American Power and the New
Mandarins* (New York: Pantheon Books, 1969), Chap. 1.
   [65] Cited by Wolf and Jorgensen, "Anthropology on the
Warpath in Thailand," from American Institutes for Research,
"Counter-insurgency in Thailand, a Research and Development
Proposal" (Pittsburgh, 1967). The report goes on to point out
that the application of the findings at home "constitutes a poten-
tially most significant project contribution."

driven from their villages by aerial bombardment to
caves in which they had lived for twelve months, "going
out only in dark clothes or at night to till their fields" in
fear of night-and-day bombing so intense that planes
"would even bomb a dog if they saw it moving," with
phosphorus bombs, which burned the houses and fruit
trees, then the fields and hillside, until "finally even the
stream was on fire"; cluster bombs, "canisters full of
deadly pellet bomblets, each one with hundreds of tiny
ball-bearings which when they explode rip human flesh";
and so on. Then finally the conclusion: it would be
wrong to mistake the "stupidity and ignorance" of the
perpetrators of these acts for "malignity"; nor should
one be driven to an "unreasoning antipathy" towards
the USSR or towards men who are not "military mon-
sters," but are thoughtful and even compassionate,
though "institutionalized" by the technical requirements
of mistaken policies.[66] How would we react to such an
account in a mildly pro-Russian journal? By reflecting
on this exercise, we may, perhaps, learn something interesting about the state of Western civilization.

Still another technique has been described by C. P.
Fitzgerald: "The mental trick of picturing the victim of
an attack in the role of the cruel and dangerous assailant
is an established mechanism for diminishing a sense of
guilt."[67] No literate Westerner will have difficulty fur-
nishing current instances.

An effective variant is to blame the victims for the

[66] Quotes and paraphrase from Ian Wright, "US in Asia—
Mad or Bad? Review of Proceedings of the Bertrand Russell War
Crimes Tribunal," *The Guardian*, January 29, 1971 (with side
remarks on my *At War with Asia*).

[67] *The Nation*, May 23, 1966. Cited by Parenti, *Anti-
Communist Impulse*, pp. 167–68.

ferocity of the attack. The Undersecretary of the Air Force writes that the rebels of Indochina are "inviting the West, which possesses unanswerable military power, to carry its strategic logic to the final conclusion, which is genocide."[68] The context, as I read it, reinforces the impression that somehow the rebels are to blame for calling this terror upon their heads. Some are more explicit. An outstanding war correspondent, strongly opposed to the war, recently summarized his feelings after a long assignment in Vietnam. The war, he writes, is a horrible mistake:

> The United States has never accepted the fundamental differentness of Vietnam—those aspects of this society that allow, for instance, its public officials to lie brazenly and daily to their American allies, or which compel beggars to buy and steal babies who might help them look more pathetic in Saigon's filthy gutters. . . . It is all too easy to forget or ignore the stupefying venality of South Vietnamese society, the selfishness of ordinary Vietnamese, the almost total lack of civic spirit in this society. . . . The fundamental American optimism about human nature can be put to a severe test in this society . . . the Vietnamese character . . . [may] . . . preclude the success of America's efforts here.[69]

And so on.

First, we destroy and demolish the rural society of Vietnam and drive millions of peasants into miserable urban slums. Then we blame them because beggars buy and steal babies who might help them look more

[68] Hoopes, *Limits of Intervention,* p. 129.

[69] Robert G. Kaiser, *Boston Globe–Washington Post,* August 30, 1970.

pathetic. It is their selfishness that puts our fundamental optimism about human nature to such a severe test—the lack of civic spirit among a people that has been fighting for twenty-five years against every horror that Western ingenuity can devise.

But the willingness to be deceived remains, surely, the major factor in explaining the remarkable lack of consciousness regarding Vietnam. Such a statement may seem strange, even perverse, given the widespread opposition to the war in the United States. But I believe that in fact the American government has won a remarkable propaganda victory, while losing all the arguments over Vietnam. It has succeeded in providing the framework within which the issues of the war are debated. Telford Taylor's book, mentioned earlier, is a good example. This can hardly be described as a "pro-government book"; in fact, he comes close to proposing war-crimes trials for American military and civilian leadership. Nevertheless, his discussion remains entirely within the framework of administration assumptions. The war, as he sees it, pits North Vietnam against South Vietnam. There is a prima-facie case that the North Vietnamese are the aggressors, given that:

> Indisputably, the ground fighting has all taken place in South Vietnam; it is the North Vietnamese who have joined the Vietcong "south of the border" and are seeking to subvert the Government of South Vietnam.[70]

But, he argues, the question whether the North or the South struck the first blow may not be significant, and an American court undertaking to judge the legality of

[70] Taylor, *Nuremberg and Vietnam*, p. 101.

our Vietnam actions would have to determine, for example, whether the North Vietnamese were justified in intervening in support of the Vietcong, given the post-Geneva history. What is remarkable in this discussion is the strict avoidance of what would appear to be the obvious question: Is the United States committing aggression in *South* Vietnam, has it violated its legal obligation to refrain from the threat or use of force in international affairs by its intervention in South Vietnam and Laos since 1954 (if not before)? After all, the ground fighting has all taken place in South Vietnam, not the United States; thus there is a prima-facie case that the Americans are the aggressors. It is South Vietnam that has been subjected to the full intensity of the American assault: bombing, defoliation, forced population removal, search-and-destroy operations, free-fire zones, the Phoenix program of political assassination and "neutralization," and so on. It is primarily South Vietnam that the United States seems to have seen "as enemy territory which can be devastated at will," where "the balance of nature . . . has been destroyed for decades to come," where "the ruthless bombardment of suspected communist positions has devastated villages and irrigation schemes—the essential capital of the peasant community." It is primarily in South Vietnam that "it is not an exaggeration to compare this situation with the vicious way the Germans fought across the Soviet Union in the second world war or the destruction wrought by the anti-Nazi allies within Germany in the final defeat of the Third Reich."[71] It is in South Vietnam

[71] "The Rape of Indochina," *Far Eastern Economic Review,* July 16, 1970, p. 22.

and Laos that the Americans concluded

> that there might be some advantage to be drawn
> . . . from the exodus caused by their bombings of
> the countryside and occupations of the towns. They
> reasoned, rightly or wrongly, that their savage
> action and its results would allow them to break
> down the traditional socio-economic structures of
> the two countries, and, more questionably, that
> they could thus put down a rebellion closely inter-
> woven with these structures.[72]

Furthermore, it is known, from United States government sources, that the American military involvement in the South was much earlier and, obviously,
always far greater in scale than that of the North Vietnamese (not to speak of the matter of legitimacy). The
Pentagon and Senator Mansfield have revealed that the
first regular North Vietnamese troops—one battalion of
400 to 500 men—were detected in South Vietnam in
late April 1965, two and a half months after the onset
of the intensive bombardment of South and North Vietnam, more than eight months after the heavy bombardment that followed the fabricated Tonkin Gulf incident.
Chester Cooper confirms this once again in his recent
memoirs:

> By the end of April [1965] it was believed that
> 100,000 Viet Cong irregulars and between 38,000
> and 46,000 main-force enemy troops, including a
> full battalion of regular North Vietnamese troops,
> were in South Vietnam. Meanwhile, American
> combat forces were moving into South Vietnam at
> a rapid rate; in late April more than 35,000

[72] Jean-Claude Pomonti, *Le Monde Weekly Selection,* September 23, 1970.

American troops had been deployed and by early May the number had increased to 45,000.

When the intensive bombing of South and North was initiated in early February, the State Department attempted to provide a justification in a White Paper claiming aggression from the North. As Cooper admits, this was "a dismal disappointment." The main problem was "that the actual findings [regarding alleged aggression] seemed pretty frail." For example, "Three 75-millimeter recoilless rifles of Chinese Communist origin, forty-six Soviet-made rifles, forty sub-machine guns and one automatic pistol of Czech origin had been captured" as compared with the $860 million in military assistance given by the United States to the Saigon government since 1961. Nor did the number of infiltrators seem large, compared with the 23,000 American troops (who, he fails to add, had been directly involved in military operations for several years). In fact, the White Paper could produce virtually no evidence of any infiltration except for South Vietnamese, returning to their homes years after the subversion of the Geneva accords.[73] (Cooper does not mention that, according to the very knowledgeable Bernard Fall, "infiltration" of Saigon army commandos to the North had begun several years prior to the alleged infiltration to the South, nor does he record the number of trained South Vietnamese "infiltrated" to the South after receiving military training in the United States or elsewhere.) In fact, United States officials in Saigon estimated in 1962 that about half the population supported the National Liberation Front, and

[73] *The Lost Crusade: America in Vietnam* (New York: Dodd, Mead & Company, 1970), pp. 277, 264, 265.

it is generally admitted that province after province had fallen to indigenous forces at the time of the outright American invasion—in fact, this was why the invasion and the intensive regular bombardment of the South seemed necessary. What is more, there is ample testimony as to why the NLF was so successful: namely, their programs appealed to the rural population.[74] This evidence is hardly obscure, and much of it derives from strongly pro-United States government sources. Yet in the face of it, Taylor sees no need to question the government claim that the war is a war between North and South, and no reason to raise the question of American aggression in the South. He is far from alone in accepting the framework of government assumptions, while challenging some of the conclusions reached within this framework of official fantasy. In connection with Laos and Cambodia, as well as other aspects of the war in Vietnam itself, many similar examples can be cited. What they demonstrate is the amazing power of state propaganda, even in a relatively open society where access to information is not limited, at least to the intellectual elite.

In the last years of his life, Russell devoted himself

[74] For evidence on these matters, see, for example, Robert Sansom, *The Economics of Insurgency in the Mekong Delta* (Cambridge, Mass.: The M.I.T. Press, 1970); William Nighswonger, *Rural Pacification in Vietnam* (New York: Praeger Publishers, 1967); Jeffrey Race, "How They Won," *Asian Survey*, August 1970 (and his excellent study of Long An province, to appear); Douglas Pike, *Viet Cong* (Cambridge, Mass.: The M.I.T. Press, 1966); and many other sources. In some of these (Pike, for example), one has to distinguish quite carefully between evidence and conclusions.

with remarkable energy to combatting state propaganda, with regard to Vietnam, the possibilities of nuclear disaster, and other matters. These efforts failed to have much impact. Official myths still largely prevail. To conclude this discussion, I will cite one final case: the missile crisis of 1962. Khrushchev, in a move so foolhardly as to defy description, secretly installed missiles in Cuba, probably in reaction to the substantial American lead in offensive weaponry. The United States government response was most remarkable. Reflecting on this crisis, Robert Kennedy observed that the fourteen people involved in determining the American response were

> bright, able, dedicated people, all of whom had the greatest affection for the United States—probably the brightest kind of group you could get together under those circumstances. If six of them had been President of the United States, I think that the world might have been blown up.[75]

These fourteen people refused to respond officially to an offer by Khrushchev to withdraw the missiles from Cuba, thus terminating the crisis, because this offer was coupled with the demand that American missiles be withdrawn from Turkey and Italy (these were obsolete missiles, for which a withdrawal order had already been given by the President). According to Sorensen's memoirs, the President believed that the probability of war was between one third and one half during the missile crisis. Yet fourteen bright and able people were

[75] An interview two days before his assassination, reported in Ronald Steel's review of Kennedy's *Thirteen Days,* "Endgame," *New York Review of Books,* March 13, 1969, p. 22.

willing to accept a high probability of nuclear war in defense of the principle that the United States alone has the right to keep missiles on the border of a potential enemy. Adam Yarmolinsky, who was then special assistant to the Secretary of Defense, relates that

> the Executive Committee of the National Security Council spent at least 90% of its time studying alternative uses of troops, bombers, and warships. Although the possibility of seeking withdrawal of the missiles by straightforward diplomatic negotiation received some attention within the State Department, it seems scarcely to have been considered by the President.[76]

In the heat of crisis, one can expect irrational decisions. (The thought, however, is not comforting.) But consider the response in calmer moments. I think that most commentators would agree with historian Thomas A. Bailey that the missile crisis was "Kennedy's finest hour," in which he "played the game of nuclear chicken with coolness and skill, thereby largely erasing the black mark of the Bay of Pigs."[77] The chairman of the Committee on International Relations at the University of Chicago, Professor Morton A. Kaplan, agrees:

> The handling of the Cuban missile crisis was John F. Kennedy's shining hour. Those who make abom-

[76] Yarmolinsky, "The Military Establishment," p. 91.

[77] "Johnson and Kennedy: The Two Thousand Days," *New York Times Magazine*, November 6, 1966, p. 139. The Vietnamese, incidentally, have little reason to be thankful for this victory. As Cooper relates, Kennedy's dramatic success gave "an added fillip" to his foreign-policy stance. This impelled him further into Southeast Asia, where "Vietnam provided both a challenge and an opportunity to test the new doctrines" of counterinsurgency.

inable criticisms of him for his handling of that crisis need to have both their heads and their hearts examined.[78]

Specifically, Kaplan is denouncing the suggestion that domestic politics played a role in Kennedy's decision,[79] though he himself agrees that this was probably the case:

> No doubt Kennedy thought of the elections. He was a politician, he had problems of regime control, and motivations are always mixed.

Referring to the missile crisis, Ronald Steel remarks, quite correctly, that what occurred shows "how slender is the thread of our survival." The conclusion is strengthened when we consider the subsequent response, as typified by the statements I have just quoted (which are, I believe, typical of a wide range of serious opinion). It has, in fact, been argued that in the same year, the Kennedy administration may also have con-

[78] Review of Robert Kennedy, *Thirteen Days,* in *Political Science Quarterly,* Vol. 85, No. 4 (December 1970), pp. 654–56.

[79] Evidence for this is summarized by Ronald Steel, in his review of the same book (see note 75 above). He cites remarks to this effect by Roger Hilsman, Dwight Eisenhower, Theodore Sorensen, John Kenneth Galbraith, and others. Kaplan, following the principle of castigating the bearer of bad tidings, comments that this idea "takes on the quality of paranoia that one expects from the *New York Review of Books,*" failing to mention that the idea is suggested, not by Steel, but in the sources cited. To compound the absurdity, he then, in the cited quotation, agrees that Kennedy no doubt had the 1962 elections in mind. Kaplan differs from Steel in believing that Kennedy's political interest and the national interest coincided.

Incidentally, since Kaplan cannot bring himself to identify the man who he feels has so defamed his leader, I can only assume that he is referring to Steel's review of the same book in the *New York Review of Books.*

sidered the use of nuclear weapons in Southeast Asia after the defeat of CIA-sponsored Lao forces who had caused a violation of the Geneva cease-fire, leading to false rumors of foreign (presumably Chinese) intervention.[80] Such examples are sufficient to demonstrate that Russell's concern over the threat of nuclear war was that of a reasonable man.

The threat persists, of course. A strong argument can be given that the "Nixon Doctrine" tends to lower the nuclear threshold.[81] In Vietnam, President Nixon has offered no alternative to "the enemy" but surrender. If they choose to continue the struggle to liberate South Vietnam (from Nixon's point of view, to conquer South Vietnam), the response will be massive,[82] and may

[80] See Jonathan Mirsky and Stephen E. Stonefield, "The United States in Laos, 1945–1962," in Edward Friedman and Mark Selden, eds., *America's Asia* (New York: Pantheon Books, 1971), pp. 253–323.

[81] See Earl C. Ravenal, "The Nixon Doctrine and Our Asian Commitments," *Foreign Affairs,* Vol. 49, No. 2 (January 1971), pp. 201–17. Ravenal was the director of the Asian Division (Systems Analysis) in the office of the Secretary of Defense, 1967–1969. See also Daniel Lang. "A Reporter at Large: The Supreme Option," *New Yorker,* January 9, 1971, pp. 52–61.

[82] For recent discussion, see Morton H. Halperin, "Vietnam: Options," *New York Times,* November 7, 1970 (Halperin recently resigned from the Senior Staff of the National Security Council); Michael Malloy, "Vietnam: Prelude to Brute Force," *Far Eastern Economic Review,* December 26, 1970. The use of tactical nuclear weapons has been discussed by Cyrus Sulzberger, *New York Times,* November 15, 1970. A recent NATO meeting discussed the utility of atomic land mines to block mountain passes and invasion routes, referring to the Turkish border, but in terms that suggest an application to Southeast Asia. (See William Beecher, *New York Times,* October 28, 1970.) Sailors from the aircraft carrier U.S.S. *Oriskany,* operat-

include tactical nuclear weapons, with consequences that are unpredictable. The two great causes to which Bertrand Russell devoted his last years—prevention of nuclear war and ending the Vietnam atrocity—may yet turn out to be a single cause, after all.

Russell's hopes for a radical transformation of the advanced industrial societies of the West to some form of libertarian socialism are as remote from realization as they were when he wrote extensively about these matters, during World War I. It is the problem of survival, not revolution, that has obsessed us: in recent years, survival for the victims of oppression and for mankind itself, as the state risks total destruction to ensure its prestige and dominance. It is proper and necessary that this should be so. Russell was, without question, justified in committing his energies, in his last years, to reversing the arms race and preventing the West from pursuing its strategic logic in Southeast Asia to the final conclusion. To resist the depredations of the great powers, in Asia, Eastern Europe, and elsewhere, and to resist the threat to survival that they pose—these are the most urgent, most compelling tasks. Yet it would be tragic if those who are fortunate enough to live in the advanced societies of the West were to forget or abandon the hope that our world can be transformed to "a world in which the creative spirit is alive, in which life is an adventure

---

ing in the Gulf of Tonkin, have told reporters that they have regular practice drills in which they load tactical nuclear weapons on the A-4 Skyhawks, small subsonic jets used regularly for the bombing of Indochina but unlikely to be employed in a war against a major power (Fred Branfman, Dispatch News Service International, Saigon, December 3, 1970).

full of hope and joy, based rather upon the impulse to construct than upon the desire to retain what we possess or to seize what is possessed by others." I have already quoted Russell's vision of the world that we must seek. I will conclude by following these remarks to their conclusion:

Meantime, the world in which we exist has other aims. But it will pass away, burned up in the fire of its own hot passions; and from its ashes will spring a new and younger world, full of fresh hope, with the light of morning in its eyes.